SAINTS BARSANUPHIUS AND JOHN:

GUIDANCE TOWARD SPIRITUAL LIFE

Orthodox Theological Texts

Saints Barsanuphius & John

GUIDANCE TOWARD SPIRITUAL LIFE

Answers to the Questions of Disciples

by
SAINTS BARSANUPHIUS AND JOHN

Selected and translated by
Fr. Seraphim Rose

ST. HERMAN OF ALASKA BROTHERHOOD
1990

†

Address all correspondence to:
St. Herman of Alaska Brotherhood
P. O. Box 70
Platina, California 96076

FIRST ENGLISH EDITION

Translated from the Russian. Original Russian edition: The Holy Fathers Barsanuphius and John, *Guidance Toward Spiritual Life (Rukovodstvo k Duchovnoi Zhizni),* Moscow, 1855.

Cover: Icon of Sts. Barsanuphius and John by Sr. Mary (Weston).
Frontispiece: 19th-century engraving of Palestine; from *Those Holy Fields* by Samuel Manning, 1874.

Library of Congress Cataloging in Publication Data

Barsanuphius and John, Saints (6th century A.D.)
   Guidance toward spiritual life: answers to the questions of disciples.
   Translated by Fr. Seraphim Rose.
   1. Christianity. 2. Patristic Theology. 3. Palestine.
   I. Title.

Library of Congress Catalog Number 88-063596
ISBN 0938-635-19-0

CONTENTS

HIEROMONK SERAPHIM ROSE
1934-1982

PREFACE

1. ABOUT THIS TRANSLATION

IN 1969, when Fr. Seraphim Rose went with his brother in Christ, Fr. Herman, to live in the mountains of northern California, he stated their aims as follows:

1. To live a monastic life as much as possible in the tradition and spirit of the Orthodox desert-dwellers of all centuries, and in particular of those nearest to us in time . . . like them, to flee from the world and all worldly understanding, in mutual obedience, in deprivation, cutting off each other's will and forcing each other on the narrow path that leads to salvation, the Brotherhood's inner life not being dependent on any organization or individual outside (in accordance with the commandment of Blessed Paisius Velichkovsky) but proceeding by mutual counsel in obedience to the eldest brother. . . .
2. To be constantly nourished spiritually by the Lives and Writings of the Holy Fathers of the Orthodox Church . . . to translate, be instructed by, and apply these writings to daily life.
3. To make known to all who thirst for it this Patristic Orthodox teaching, most especially by the printed word, and to encourage and inspire others to base their Christian lives on this foundation.

During the first few years of their life in the forest, Fathers Seraphim and Herman were able to pursue these aims without distractions. Few visitors came to their remote and unknown hermitage. This period of almost total isolation was necessary for them to "soak in" the writings of the Holy Fathers and the ancient cycle of church services, to enter deeply into the timeless Orthodox way of life.

But the fathers could not remain in their voluntary hiding forever. By 1973, their small "St. Herman Hermitage" had become a center of interest in church circles, and monastic aspirants began to arrive. Up to this time, the fathers had sought to guide and help people only through their printed articles; but now they were called upon to take direct and personal responsibility for the salvation of young souls. Knowing from their own fathers in the faith that the ancient Orthodox practice of *eldership* was not given to our times, they did not want to outwardly "mimic" the early desert fathers or set themselves up as authorities on spiritual life. At the same time, they knew that the definite principles of Christian life taught by the Holy Fathers must be followed by believers of all times and places if they are to save their souls.

One of these principles, Fr. Seraphim understood, was that "trusting oneself" is almost guaranteed to lead to ruin. While the monastic aspirants of the St. Herman Hermitage could not look at Fr. Seraphim as a "God-bearing Elder" and submit to him as such, neither could they be their own personal authorities. They had to form a relationship of mutual trust and openness with their spiritual father, avoiding the opposite extremes of idolizing and "knowing better" than one's guide.

Not trusting oneself was no less important for the teacher than it was for the pupil. Fr. Seraphim therefore avoided offering his own opinions. He wanted the Holy Fathers to say what had to be said, and not he himself. Nor was he content to rely on his own interpretation of what the Holy

Fathers taught. He always referred to the interpretations offered by reliable teachers of recent centuries[1] and by his own living spiritual fathers and mothers,[2] from whom he had directly received the Orthodox teaching on spiritual life as passed down from antiquity in an unbroken line.

At one point there were fourteen persons living at the hermitage, each with his own problems and needs. The new brothers were all products of modern American society, with its emphasis on individualism and the gratification of the self, on the "do what makes you happy" philosophy. Before Fr. Seraphim lay the task of passing on to the brothers, so spoiled and pampered by their upbringing, a way of life totally different from that of the world. Now that they had chosen to serve God, he had to give them the Patristic teaching on how to conduct community life in a monastery, on how to no longer live for themselves.

With this in mind, he set out to translate classic Patristic expositions into English. One of these was *Guidance Toward Spiritual Life* by Saints Barsanuphius the Great and John the Prophet, desert ascetics of 6th-century Palestine. Beginning in 1973, Fr. Seraphim selected and translated from this work passages which he felt best spoke to the needs of the particular brothers who were at the hermitage at that time. He would read these aloud at meals in the refectory—very slowly, so that each word would sink in.

For years, until after Fr. Seraphim's death in 1982, the translation of *Guidance Toward Spiritual Life* existed only in handwritten form, included in the pages of Fr. Seraphim's "spiritual journal." Together with it were translations of other Patristic passages which Fr. Seraphim found particular-

---

1. St. Ignatius Brianchaninov, St. Theophan the Recluse, St. Paisius Velichkovsky, Elder Theodore of Sanaxar, the Elders of Valaam and Optina Monasteries, etc.

2. Blessed Archbishop John Maximovitch, Archbishop Averky of Jordanville, Archimandrite Spyridon Efimov, Ivan and Helen Kontzevitch, Schemamonk Nikodim of Mount Athos, and others.

ly meaningful: from the writings of St. Macarius the Great, St. Symeon the New Theologian, St. Paisius Velichkovsky and St. John of Kronstadt. His translation of portions of the *Spiritual Homilies* of St. Macarius the Great have been appended to this edition.

Fr. Seraphim found that many of the questions posed to Saints Barsanuphius and John in *Guidance Toward Spiritual Life* are not unlike those asked by Christian strugglers of today; and the answers of the Elders cut right through common fantasies and misconceptions. They expose the nature of the vices—feigned humility, cold-hearted calcula- tion, judgment, idleness, lack of inward vigilance, carnal thoughts, vainglory—and show the way to overcome them and acquire virtue. From the Elders' words one can learn of the remarkable subtlety of demonic deception, and become aware of the painstaking carefulness with which a Christian must examine all his thoughts, words and deeds to see if they are of God. The love of elder for disciple comes through in every passage. It is apparent that the Elders do not care to exert personal power over those under them: with divine vision they see the eternal souls of their disciples; and the salvation of these souls is their one and only concern in offering guidance.

Fr. Seraphim did his translation from the Russian edition of *Guidance Toward Spiritual Life*, published in 1855 by Optina Monastery. The first 137 chapters of this book were included in the Russian *Philokalia (Dobrotolubie)* by the modern Holy Father St. Theophan the Recluse (†1894), and have already appeared in English.[3] Only the present English translation, however, contains selections from the complete edition of 850 chapters.

---

3. *Writings from the Philokalia on Prayer of the Heart* (Faber and Faber, London, 1951), pp. 346-381.

2. HUMILITY

Fr. Seraphim constantly counselled the brethren to always be humbling themselves down, cutting off their personal whims and passions, "squashing" themselves before their brothers, asking forgiveness with contrition of heart. Many passages in *Guidance Toward Spiritual Life* describe this kind of genuine humility, and Fr. Seraphim tended to select these in doing his translation. He was always watchful not to let himself or his brothers get puffed up with thoughts of their own "spirituality" or "Patristic wisdom." "We must come to the Holy Fathers," he wrote, "with the humble intention of *beginning spiritual life at the lowest step,* and not even dreaming of ourselves attaining those exalted spiritual states which are totally beyond us." In his now-classic series of articles on the Holy Fathers, Fr. Seraphim drew from the teachings of Saints Barsanuphius and John in showing how we are to approach the Patristic writings with "the fear of God, with humility, and with a great distrust of our own wisdom and judgment." He wrote:

"To aid our humble intention in reading the Holy Fathers, we must begin with the elementary Patristic books, those which teach the 'ABC's.' A 6th-century novice of Gaza once wrote to the great clairvoyant Elder, St. Barsanuphius, much in the spirit of the inexperienced Orthodox student of today: 'I have dogmatic books and when reading them I feel that my mind is transferred from passionate thoughts to the contemplation of dogmas.' To this the holy Elder replied: 'I would not want you to be occupied with these books, because they exalt the mind on high; but it is better to study the words of the Elders which humble the mind downward. I have said this not in order to belittle the dogmatic books, but I only give you counsel; for foods are different.' (*Answers to the Questions of Disciples,* no. 544). . . .

"Again, different Patristic books on the spiritual life are suitable for Orthodox Christians in different conditions of life: that which is suitable especially for solitaries is not directly applicable to monks living the common life; that which applies to monks in general will not be directly relevant for laymen; and in every condition, the spiritual food which is suitable for those with some experience may be entirely indigestible for beginners. Once one has achieved a certain balance in spiritual life by means of active practice of God's commandments within the discipline of the Orthodox Church, by fruitful reading of the more elementary writings of the Holy Fathers, and by spiritual guidance from living fathers—then one can receive much spiritual benefit from all the writings of the Holy Fathers, applying them to one's own condition of life. Bishop Ignatius Brianchaninov[4] has written concerning this: 'It has been noticed that novices can never adapt books to their own condition, but are invariably drawn by the tendency of the book. If a book gives counsels on silence and shows the abundance of spiritual fruits that are gathered in profound silence, the beginner invariably has the strongest desire to go off into solitude, to an uninhabited desert. If a book speaks of unconditional obedience under the direction of a Spirit-bearing Father, the beginner will inevitably develop a desire for the strictest life in complete submission to an Elder. God has not given to our time either of these two ways of life. But the books of Holy Fathers describing these states can influence a beginner so strongly that out of inexperience and ignorance he can easily decide to leave the place where he is living and where he has every convenience to work out his salvation and make spiritual progress by putting into practice the evangelical commandments, for an impossible dream of a perfect life pictured vividly and alluringly in his imagination.' Therefore, he concludes: 'Do not trust your thoughts, opinions, dreams, impulses or inclinations, even though they offer you or put before you in an attractive guise the most holy monastic life' (*The Arena*, ch. 10). What Bishop Ignatius says here about

---

4. A modern-day Russian Holy Father, reposed in 1867.

monks refers also to laymen, with allowance made for the different conditions of lay life. . . .

"St. Barsanuphius indicates in another Answer (no. 62) something else very important for us who approach the Holy Fathers much too academically: 'One who is taking care for his salvation should not at all ask [the Elders, i.e., read Patristic books] for the acquiring only of knowledge, for "knowledge puffeth up" (I Cor. 8:1), as the Apostle says; but it is most fitting to ask about the passions and about how one should live one's life, that is, how to be saved; for this is necessary, and leads to salvation.' Thus, one is not to read the Holy Fathers out of mere curiosity or as an academic exercise, without the active intention to practice what they teach, according to one's spiritual level. Modern academic 'theologians' have clearly enough demonstrated that it is possible to have much abstract information about the Holy Fathers without any spiritual knowledge at all. Of such ones St. Macarius the Great says (Homily 17:9): 'Just as one clothed in beggarly garments might see himself in sleep as a rich man, but on waking from sleep sees himself poor and naked, so also those who deliberate about the spiritual life seem to speak logically, but inasmuch as that of which they speak is not verified in the mind by any kind of experience, power, and confirmation, they remain in a kind of fantasy.'

"One test of whether our reading of the Holy Fathers is academic or real is indicated by St. Barsanuphius in his answer to a novice who found that he became haughty and proud when speaking of the Holy Fathers (Answer no. 697): 'When you converse about the life of the Holy Fathers and their Answers, you should condemn yourself, saying: Woe is me! How can I speak of the virtues of the Fathers, while I myself have acquired nothing like that and have not advanced at all? And I live, instructing others for their benefit; how can there not be fulfilled in me the word of the Apostle: "Thou that teachest another, teachest thou not thyself?"' "

(Rom. 2:21.) Thus, one's constant attitude toward the teaching of the Holy Fathers must be one of *self-reproach.*

"Finally, we must remember that the whole purpose of reading the Holy Fathers is, not to give us some kind of 'spiritual enjoyment' or confirm us in our own righteousness or superior knowledge or 'contemplative' state, but solely to aid us in the practice of the active path of virtue. Many of the Holy Fathers discuss the distinction between the 'active' and the 'contemplative' (or, more properly, 'noetic') life, and it should be emphasized here that this does not refer, as some might think, to any artificial distinction between those leading the 'ordinary' life of 'outward Orthodoxy' or mere 'good deeds,' and an 'inward' life cultivated only by monastics or some intellectual elite; not at all. There is only one Orthodox spiritual life, and it is lived by every Orthodox struggler, whether monastic or layman, whether beginner or advanced; 'action' or 'practice' (*praxis* in Greek) is the way, and 'vision' (*theoria*) or 'deification' is the end. Almost all the Patristic writings refer to the life of *action,* not the life of *vision;* when the latter is mentioned, it is to remind us of the goal of our labors and struggles, which in this life is tasted only by a few of the great Saints, but in its fullness is known only in the age to come. Even the most exalted writings of the *Philokalia,* as Bishop Theophan the Recluse wrote in the preface of the final volume of the Russian-language *Philokalia,* 'have had in view not the noetic, but almost exclusively the active life.' "5

3. PAIN OF HEART

While translating *Guidance Toward Spiritual Life,* Fr. Seraphim wrote down the following partial list of subjects which he thought were especially vital for Orthodox Chris-

5. *The Orthodox Word* (St. Herman Brotherhood, Platina, California), 1975, no. 60, pp. 38-40.

tians of today. These subjects are followed by the numbers of chapters in which they appear:

1. Fake humility and true—how to test it: Nos. 17, 37, 79, 152, 153, 156, 161, 188, 274, 275.
2. What comes from God is calm; what comes from the devil is with disturbance: Nos. 21, 59, 330, 402, 452, 470, 471, 731.
3. Don't ask questions just for knowledge—but on how to save your soul: Nos. 62, 544.
4. To struggle "according to one's strength": Nos. 84, 169, 342, 711. Struggling—against bodily repose: Nos. 124, 132, 133, 540.
5. Sorrows, slanders, etc., for testing: Nos. 109, 141, 165, 187, 196, 197, 404, 493.
6. Pain of heart (this is what separates crazy converts and careless Orthodox from true strugglers): Nos. 262, 263, 264.

Fr. Seraphim's comments on this last subject, *pain of heart,* reveal just how significant he felt it to be. Besides its fully intended literal meaning, pain of heart may more generally refer to an elemental inward suffering, the bearing of an interior cross while following Jesus Christ. It is actually a kind of watershed of true spiritual life. St. Barsanuphius said that "every gift is received through pain of heart." And in the words of the 4th-century anchorite, St. Mark the Ascetic, "Remembrance of God is *pain of heart,* endured in the spirit of devotion; but he who forgets God becomes self-indulgent and insensitive." This precise spiritual law is most clearly manifested in our own times. Fr. Seraphim explained as follows:

"The Patristic teaching on *pain of heart* is one of the most important teachings for our days when 'head-knowledge' is so much overemphasized at the expense of the proper development of emotional and spiritual life. . . . The lack of this essential experience is what above all is responsible for the dilettantism, the triviality, the want of seriousness in the ordinary study of the Holy Fathers today; without it, one

ST. MARK THE ASCETIC
4th century
Commemorated April 5

Icon by Photios Kontoglou, from the church
of St. Nicholas in Acharenon, Athens.

cannot apply the teachings of the Holy Fathers to one's own life. One may attain to the very highest level of understanding with the mind of the teaching of the Holy Fathers, may have 'at one's fingertips' quotes from the Holy Fathers on every conceivable subject, may have 'spiritual experiences' which *seem* to be those described in the Patristic books, may even know perfectly all the pitfalls into which it is possible to fall in spiritual life—and still, without pain of heart, one can be a barren fig tree, a boring 'know-it-all' who is always 'correct,' or an adept in all the present-day 'charismatic' experiences, who does not know and cannot convey the true spirit of the Holy Fathers."[6]

Fr. Seraphim's warnings against spiritual high-mindedness, his emphasis on struggle and suffering, were an attempt to make people aware that the study of the Holy Fathers is a very serious matter which should not be taken lightly, according to the intellectual and religious fashions of our times. "But this warning," he wrote, "should not frighten away the serious Orthodox Christian. The reading of the Holy Fathers is, indeed, an indispensable thing for one who values his salvation and wishes to work it out with fear and trembling; but one must come to this reading in a *practical* way so as to make maximum use of it."[7]

—Fr. Damascene
Exaltation of the Cross, 1990

---

6. *Ibid.,* no. 65, p. 239.
7. *Ibid.*

STS. BARSANUPHIUS THE GREAT AND JOHN THE PROPHET
Monks of Gaza, Palestine in the 6th century.
Commemorated February 6

Icon courtesy of Holy Transfiguration Monastery.

The Life of Our Holy Fathers
BARSANUPHIUS
AND JOHN

by
ST. NICODEMUS OF MOUNT ATHOS
Compiler of the Greek *Philokalia*

From the Russian edition of Guidance Toward
Spiritual Life *(Moscow, 1855), pp. i-xxviii. The chapter
titles have been supplied by the translators.*

1. THE HONEY OF SILENCE

THE WRITERS of this God-wise and soul-profiting book were truly God-bearing, Christ-bearing and Spirit-bearing Fathers—Barsanuphius and John— examples of asceticism, practitioners of hesychasm, lamps of discernment, sleepless eyes of clairvoyance, treasuries of virtues, and embodiments of the Holy Spirit.

But time, that crushes everything good and covers with the darkness of forgetfulness, has not left for us a narrative of the lives of these God-bearing luminaries, Barsanuphius and John. Therefore I, the infirm one, have attempted to extract,

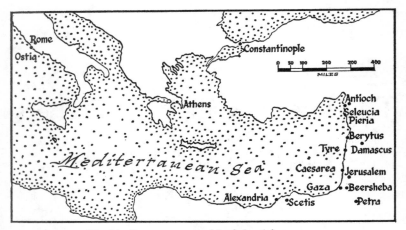

The Mediterranean world of the 6th century,
the time of Saints Barsanuphius and John.

from this their own book, several passages which witness
about their lives, and to present them to those who wish to
know what virtues these God-bearing Fathers attained—this
extreme perfection, accessible to mortals.

The great and divine Father Barsanuphius was born in
Egypt, as Evagrius the scholar testifies in the 32nd chapter
of his fourth book of Church History. From the 55th Answer
of the Elder himself, it is evident that he was learned in the
Egyptian and Helleno-Greek languages. This memorable
man from early years strove to conduct an ascetic life. Once,
passing by a place of horse racing, where people together
with irrational animals throw themselves into the compe-
tition, and seeing there how one strove to overcome and out-
run another, he said mentally to himself: "See how diligently the servants of the demons are laboring. Shouldn't
we, the inheritors of the heavenly kingdom, labor even
harder?" And having become, thanks to this showplace,
even more enthusiastic, St. Barsanuphius embraced *podvig*
(spiritual labor), as the other Elder, John, writes about
him in Answer 450. Having come to the region of Gaza

22

A rare 17th-century engraving of Gaza, Palestine,
where Saints Barsanuphius and John lived.

in Palestine, and having found there the coenobitic monastery of Abbot Seridos, he built himself a little cell, at first outside of the monastery. Secluding himself in it, he enjoyed silence like the most sweet honey, as is seen from Answer 221. It seems that he also built himself another cell in which to be a recluse, and secluded himself in it also; but where he built it is not known. One can only surmise that it was in the vicinity of the monastery.

2. DEATH TO THE PASSIONS

At the beginning of his silence, they used to bring him only three loaves of bread a week from the monastery, with which he sustained himself (Answer 72). At the same time he would give himself over to weeping; and he derived such sweetness from tears that from the experience of this unexplainable sweetness he was satisfied with a little bread alone. He would often forget to partake even of this, in accordance with the words of David: "I am smitten like grass, and withered is my heart, for I forgot to eat my bread" (Ps. 101:5). At times he would partake of food twice a week. Sometimes, coming for a meal, he would approach the food as if already filled; and when he would partake of it he would reproach himself, saying: "Why am I always not in such a state?" From the sweetness of spiritual food he would forget the physical (Answer 96). And what is more amazing is that he could have been in such a state his whole life—not partaking of food and drink, and not clothing himself in garments—because his food, drink, and clothing were the Holy Spirit (Answer 78).

In the course of time, washing himself in constant prayers, the blessed one cleansed his heart—not only from bodily passions, but also from spiritual passions: self-opinion, vainglory, man-pleasing, cunning, and other similar things which are even more hidden in the heart. In this way he rose above the enemies' arrows and acquired peace of thoughts—which is the embodiment of the gift of the Holy Spirit, as the divine Gregory of Thessalonica says in his homily to Nun Xenia: "He has acquired that which in him was dormant; that is, all passionate movement and passionate thinking has died." And that is why he called his seclusion his grave. The other Elder, John, when answering the question of why the Great Elder called his cell thus, explained: "It was because he died to all passions, for he was absolutely dead to sin. And his cell, into which he secluded himself as if in a grave for the Name of Jesus, is a place of repose where no demon enters, nor the prince of demons—the devil. It became his light-bearing chamber wherein was the abode of God" (Answer 73). From that very time, he purified his heart from passions and became worthy of being a temple and dwelling-place of the Holy Spirit. As a result of such purity, he became enriched with a most creative, true and perfect humility—not that external humility which consists of humble clothing and humble words, but that which, according to the word of the great Gregory of Thessalonica (see his homily to Nun Xenia), is erected by the Holy Spirit: "Create in me a clean heart, O God, and renew a right spirit within me" (Ps. 50:10). That is why the Fathers, and especially the divine Gregory of Sinai, call this humbleness a God-given one. Humility, according to the word of Barsanuphius himself, consists of considering oneself as earth and ashes in deed and not in words alone, so as to be able to say: "Who am I, and who considers me to be something? I have no doings with anyone" (Answer 191). By such humility the Great Elder acquired the greatest of all virtues—discernment, which, according to the word of this same Barsanuphius, is given to a monk from God as a rudder.

3. THE GIFT OF PROPHECY

According to the word of the Blessed Meletius the Confessor: "Discernment is the ascent of virtues, the beginning, the middle and the end of all good. It is a lamp shining in the darkness, a pathfinder for the lost ones, and a harbor for the storm-tossed" (Step 166). From discernment, the great Barsanuphius became worthy to acquire foresight, through which, according to the explanation of St. Peter Damascene, noetic and mystical essences are perceived by sentient and rational beings.

By way of foresight, St. Barsanuphius was vouchsafed to receive the gifts of clairvoyance and prophecy, in order to see what was occurring at a distance as if it was nearby, and the future as if present. This gift was given to this blessed Father in such abundance that he, two years in advance, foreknew and foretold the arrival of a monk from St. Sabbas Monastery into their community of St. John the Baptist (Answer 1). He also foreknew and foretold that certain rich people would come into the monastery and would remain there to live (Answer 31). He also knew, by means of grace, the attitude of people's hearts, and would answer their questions not in conformity with their words, but according to the direction of their mind and thoughts (Answers 64, 161). And his prophecies were confirmed by experience. Thus he prophesied about a prince who was sent from the king to be placed on the throne of Gaza as an unworthy bishop: "Although this bishop will reach the city gates, he will not enter the city because God will not permit it." And truly this is what happened. A message was received unexpectedly about the death of the king, and all of the hopes and plans of the bishop were destroyed (Answer 812).

4. THE FLAME OF LOVE

Who is in a condition to depict the abundant love of this blessed one towards God? He bore in his heart a love for Christ that was burning like a most powerful fiery flame, as he himself witnesses (Answer 109). That is why nothing could bring him to a fall—because love, according to the Apostolic statement, "never faileth" (I Cor. 13:8). And according to the words of the divine Barsanuphius, "perfect love never falters, and he who has acquired it with warmth becomes inflamed with love towards God and neighbor." Who will explain the love towards his neighbor that was burning in him? This heart-loving Father never ceased to beg God day and night that He would make all of the brethren God-bearing. Let us listen to his own words about this: "I, even before you ask me (because there is burning within me, like a mighty fiery flame, a love towards Christ Who said: 'Love thy neighbor as thyself' [Matt. 19:19]—and I am inflamed with it, burning in spirit) do not cease day and night to beg God that He will make you God-bearers, that He will make His abode in you, and move within you, and will send down upon you the Holy Spirit. . . . I have been like a father to you, as one who has striven to enclose his children within the light-bearing regiments of the King without their own concern" (Answer 109). And the Elder not only prayed about this to God, but actually labored that the brothers would become God-bearing and Spirit-bearing. The Great Elder also enlightened Seridos, the Abbot of the monastery, by his prayers, and opened up his mind to perceive that which was not understandable (Answer 10). Also through his prayers, the Holy Spirit descended upon St. Andrew in order to strengthen him in patience and thanksgiving (Answer 211). For his prayers reached to God as the brilliance of lightning and as the rays of the sun; so that through them the Father was gladdened, the Son rejoiced, and the Holy Spirit was comforted (Answer 110). And in all profitable petitions his prayers were heard.

Becoming more inflamed with love for his neighbor, this heavenly man, imitating Christ, would lay down his soul for his brethren, and would answer to God for them (Answers 57, 58), because he would see and cover the sins of men just as God sees and covers them (Answer 236).

5. POWER TO BIND AND LOOSE

Because of such an abundance of love towards his neighbor, he was given, directly from God, power to bind and loose sins (Answer 207), which constitutes the perfection of gifts as St. Barsanuphius himself says: "The perfection of gifts is to forgive sins, to free souls from darkness, and to lead them out into the light" (Answer 207). That is why the Lord gave the Apostles various gifts before His Resurrection, but gave this perfection of gifts to them after the Resurrection, according to the words of the same Barsanuphius: "Search the Gospels to see in which way and how many times Christ gave His disciples the gifts of healing and exorcism, and when He gave them the perfection of gifts—the power to forgive sins. He said: 'Whose soever sins ye remit, they will be forgiven' (John 20:23)" (Answer 10).

Since the great Barsanuphius was vouchsafed to receive this gift to forgive sins, he said to one certain sick brother in the monastery who asked him to forgive his sins: "God, the Great King, is saying to you, all thy sins are forgiven thee" (Answer 44). Another time he said to a different brother who was sick with tuberculosis: "According to your plea, God has forgiven you all your sins from your youth on, even unto the present time. May God be blessed Who wished to forgive you everything" (Answer 146). Sometimes the Elder would take upon himself half of the sins of certain brethren, and sometimes the whole burden of them (Answers 163, 164, 236). For certain ones he would labor, imploring God to erase the sin of their blasphemy: "Hold your lips, that you will not fall again into a worse blasphemy, although you really should not have given your soul for that. I poured out a lot of sweat imploring God for you" (Answer 228). The Great Elder would give over the souls of certain dying brethren to the Holy Life-Giving Trinity, and while they would be passing over to Heaven, he would free them from demonic attacks [tollhouses] (Answer 145). In a word, the great Barsanuphius reached that measure of love for his neighbor which the Apostle Paul had—and before Paul, the great God-seer Moses. Barsanuphius himself would pronounce the very words of Moses, as he himself writes: "Believe me, brother, that my spirit fervently compels me to say to my Master, Who rejoices over the salvation of His slaves: 'O Master, either lead me, together with my children into Thy Kingdom, or erase me out of Thy book' " (Answer 110).

6. SPIRITUAL ASCENT

Should we say more? The blessed Barsanuphius, according to the words of the divine David, made in his heart the sacred ascent, and joined humility to humility, silence to silence, and love to love. He was finally vouchsafed to reach the highest gift, which is being transported to God in order to ascend to the Seventh Heaven—not on the illusory wings of thought, but in the unutterable power of the Spirit—there to receive blessing, and to see unutterable goodness, and the mysteries of the Kingdom of God, not knowing whether he was in the body or outside of it, similar to the great Paul (II Cor. 12:3). Let us listen now to what the great Barsanuphius himself says about it: "God will assure you that love transports those who have it to the Seventh Heaven, since certain people with daring are already ascending and being blessed there, 'whether in the body, or out of the body, I cannot tell: God knoweth' (II Cor. 12:3). And in order for you to know the beginning of the way to this joy, listen to this. At first, the Holy Spirit comes to a man and teaches him everything, including how it is necessary to be wise in humility, about which you cannot hear now. You are being instructed with this the first inspiration— to ascend to the first Heaven, then to the Second, and so on to the measure of attainment, even to the Seventh— there to be vouchsafed to see unutterable and awesome things of which no one can hear except those who have reached such a measure. May the Lord vouchsafe us worthy also" (Answer 109).

7. THE POWER OF PRAYER

Thus we see why he [Barsanuphius] was given the abundant gift of miracle-working, by which he could raise the dead by the Name of our Lord Jesus Christ, chase out demons, heal incurable diseases, perform other mighty works and miracles, and, like Elias, bind and loose the heavens; as the great Barsanuphius himself says—or, more precisely, as God, Who gave him these gifts, witnesses (see Answer 181).[1]

---

1. Question 181 to the same great Elder: I believe that whatever you bind on earth will be bound in Heaven, and whatever you release on earth will be released in Heaven (Matt. 18:18). I implore you, my Father, by the mercies of God, help my infirmity. I am infirm in soul and body, and I am burdening the brothers with whom I live. Acquire strength for me from God, that I might fulfill my own obligation, and that the brothers will not have to carry my burden. I believe

The great Barsanuphius delivered from sickness an elder who lived in the monastery and who was suffering (Answers 172, 173). In a similar way he healed another sick brother (Answers 512, 513). After all this, the Great Elder was vouchsafed not only to be a son of God according to grace, but also that which is more worthy of wonder —to be called and to be a brother of Jesus, as he himself says: "Pray for me, a sinner, that I to the end will remain in such a measure. He who has attained it has already become numbered among the brethren of Jesus" (Answer

that God will give you everything—whatever you ask of Him. Be compassionate to my weakness and forgive me, my Father.

Answer 181: Your key, brother, opens my door because I am a mad man and cannot conceal the miracles of God. Therefore, whoever hears these words will be shocked and will say: "He is out of his mind and does not know what he is saying." I think that for God everything is possible (Matt. 19:26), and nothing is impossible for Him (Job 10:13; 42:2). As He acted through the Ancient Ones, raising the paralytics and resurrecting the dead Tabitha, so also can He act through contemporary slaves of His. I speak before Him and do not lie, that I know one slave of God in our generation, in this very time and in this blessed place, who can also resurrect the dead by the Name of our Lord Jesus Christ, and chase demons away, and heal incurable diseases, and do other miracles no less than those of the Apostles. He Who gave him this gift, or more precisely, these gifts, witnesses. And what does this mean in comparison with that which can be accomplished in the Name of Jesus Christ? But he did not use his own authority, although he can stop warfare, and bind and loose Heaven like Elias. Our Lord always has His faithful slaves, Whom He does not call anymore slaves—but sons. And although the enemy envies them, because of the grace of Christ he can in no way harm them. For the ship has already passed through the storm, the soldier—the battle, the rudder—bad winds, the farmer—winters, the storekeeper—thieves; and the monk has reached perfection in his solitude. Hearing such proud words, who will not say that I am mad? But in truth, I speak as if in madness; for I do not witness of myself, but of another. And if someone will think of saying: "He went mad" (as I have already said), let him so speak. But he who

181). And when his own brother in the world, in old age, wanted to talk with him, the Saint answered: "I have a brother—Jesus. If you, disdaining the world, will become a monk, then you will be a brother to me" (Answer 345).

When the divine Barsanuphius reached such perfection, he received such great daringness toward God that he alone could implore God for a numberless multitude of people; and his petitions were not turned down (see Answer 110). Therefore, when during the lifetime of this divine Father, great wrath of God came upon the whole world, the hesychastic followers in that monastery asked the holy Elder to make prayer to God

---

wants to strive zealously in order to reach such a measure (of spiritual maturity), let him not be lazy. I have said this to your love in order to assure you that what you desire is possible. For if God, according to your prayers, has foreordained heavenly good things for you, unutterable and eternal (which the "eye hath not seen, nor ear heard, neither have entered into the heart of man, the things which God hath prepared for them that love Him" [I Cor. 2:9]), and if you will receive them, having preserved what was commanded of you, then all the more is it not difficult to implore God about bodily suffering and to receive grace, so that not even a day would you be sick and feel its burden. But Jesus knows better than we what is good for the man, and what precisely helps him: so that one will receive reward for his endurance, like Job, and another for his obedience, like Eulogius the Scholar. Do not ask anything from God through His slaves, except for help and patience. "He that endureth to the end shall be saved" (Matt. 10:22) in Christ Jesus our Lord. He takes care of us (I Peter 5:7) forever, Amen. Or do you not know what the Lord said to the holy Paul, when he asked to be relieved of his sorrow? "My grace is sufficient for thee" (II Cor. 12:9). How did He say this—out of lack of love toward him, or knowing it would be of benefit to him? Remember that "the sufferings of this present time are not worthy to be compared with the glory which shall be revealed in us" (Rom. 8:18). Forgive me and pray for me a sinner, that I, even to the end, will continue in the same measure. He who has attained it has already become numbered among the brethren of Jesus, to Whom be glory forever, Amen. (1855 Edition: Moscow.)

that His wrath would cease. He answered that three perfect men were begging God for the whole world, (one of these being the great Barsanuphius himself). Here are the Saint's own words: "Many are imploring God's mercy towards men that the wrath of God on the world will cease; and there is no one more man-loving than God. But in spite of all that, He does not want to pardon us because many sins are performed in the world that oppose it. There are three men, perfect before God, who have transcended the measure of humanness and received power to loose and bind: to remit sins and retain them. It is they who stand between perdition and the world, so that the Lord does not destroy the whole world suddenly. By their prayers, He softens the punishment according to His mercy; they were told that the wrath would last for a short time. Pray with them. The prayers of these three men are met at the entry of the high sacrificial altar of the Father of Lights, and they are rejoicing and are jubilant to each other in the heavens. When they, however, look down upon the earth, then they weep together and shed tears and sob because of the evils that are performed upon it which evoke God's wrath. These men are: John in Rome, Elias in Corinth and a certain one in the Jerusalem diocese (that is, Barsanuphius himself, who is saying this, for he was a recluse near Gaza in the Jerusalem diocese). And I believe that they cause the world great good; truly so, Amen" (Answer 566).

The Saints who have received grace from God become sanctified not only in their mind and soul, but also in their holy bodies. By means of the soul they receive grace and sanctification. Thus it was with St. Barsanuphius: not only were his soul and mind penetrated with grace and enlightened, but his blessed body was also vouchsafed divine grace and sanctity. Even objects which were close to the Saint received certain divine power and grace, according to what is said in the Book of Acts—the clothes and garments of Paul healed the sick: "Even from the clothes of his body, pieces of garments were brought and laid on the sick" (Acts 19:12). So also the cowl of the great Barsanuphius, which was sent by him to John in the Monastery of St. Sabbas, protected the latter from many temptations and evils (Answer 1). Another Holy Father sent his cowl to the great Barsanuphius, asking him to wear it, thereby blessing it, and then to return it to him so that he could have in it protection and help (Answer 123). Many received other blessings from St. Barsanuphius: a morsel of bread that he ate, a bit of water that he drank. Partaking of it they felt an easing of the passions with which they were attacked (see Answers 43, 44, 169). But even the name of Abba Barsanuphius itself, even mentally evoked, was effective and gave help to those who called upon it, as the other Elder, the divine John, said to the monastery's Abbot, Elian. In answer to his question, "What kind of answer should one give to each question?" Elder John said, "Ask mentally the holy Elder: 'Abba what should I say?' and according to the Lord's commandment (Matt. 10:19) do not worry about how or what you will speak" (see Answer 592).

8. TEMPTATIONS

Such great gifts was he vouchsafed to receive, and such a great state of perfection of virtues did he attain—our great among the Fathers, Barsanuphius. However, such great gifts were achieved in him due to such temptations which many not only cannot endure in deed, but cannot even comprehend them in hearing of them. Listen to how he writes about himself in his epistle to John of St. Sabbas Monastery: "If I were to write to you about those temptations which I have endured, I think that your hearing would not endure it, and perhaps no one's in the present time" (Answer 13). Equally great were the infirmities and sicknesses to which this most blessed one was subjected. But he endured them with such valor that, being sick, he not only did not lay down sometimes on his bed for rest, but even

did not abandon his handiwork (Answer 165). He right-
eously allowed these sicknesses to assail him, since for
great gifts Saints are subjected to great temptations. And
he who does not shed blood cannot receive the Holy Spirit,
as Peter Damascene said: "Give blood, and receive Spirit."

9. GOD PRESERVES THE ELDER'S SILENCE

This Holy Father lived in the 6th century, during the time
of Emperor Justinian. Before the year 600 A.D., and for the
course of 50 years and more, not one man saw him,[2] because he locked himself in a rather small cell as if in some
grave. And in the course of this time he partook of no
other food than bread and water. When the news about this
reached Eustochius, Patriarch of Jerusalem, he did not believe it and wished to personally see the holy Barsanuphius.
For this purpose he took with him certain people, and
brought them to the place of the Saint's reclusion. When
they attempted to dig under the wall and to enter the cell
from underneath, suddenly fire burst out from there and
almost burned Eustochius himself and those with him.
Evagrius the Scholar bears witness, in the 34th chapter of
the 4th book of his Church History, saying this about him:
"During that time there were God-bearing men who would
perform great signs. Among them was the especially renowned
Barsanuphius, a native of Egypt. He lived in the flesh as
if he were fleshless, in a monastery near the city of Gaza,
and worked many miracles. He spent his life as a recluse
in a small cell, and in the course of 50 and more years would
not show himself to anybody, and did not use anything
earthly.[3] When Eustochius, the presiding hierarch of Jeru-

---

2. Except for Abbot Seridos, through whom he gave his answers,
and a few others to whom he once showed himself (see Answer 60).

3. In the course of all this time, when the great Barsanuphius stayed
in his reclusion, only once did he expose himself to certain people.
One brother, not believing that the Elder was alive, used to say that

salem, not believing this, ordered men to dig under the cell in which the man of God had enclosed himself, suddenly fire burst out of there, and almost burned all those who were there." After the repose of the great Barsanuphius, when he went to the Fathers and his longed-for Christ, then an elder who lived in the monastery (Euthymius the Silent) was placed into his grave, as the divine Barsanuphius himself had prophesied during his lifetime (Answer 152).

10. THE GOOD BARSANUPHIUS AND THE BAD BARSANUPHIUS

It is important to know that there were two Barsanuphii. One was this holy and Orthodox Father. The other one, however, was a heretic, who held to the heresy of the Monophysites. [Followers of this heresy] were called "headless," and "ten-horned ones," because they considered not some one person, but many, as the founders of this heresy. Divine Sophronius, Patriarch of Jerusalem, entered that heretic Barsanuphius into the book which contained confessions of the Faith[4] and which he sent to those who were assembled at the 6th Ecumenical Council against the Monothelites.

This divine Barsanuphius about whom we are writing was a man absolutely Orthodox in everything, and the Church of Christ venerates him as a saint. This was confirmed by the holy Patriarch Tarasius, when he was asked about this by St. Theodore the Studite. And this was witnessed by St. Theodore the Studite himself in his testament, in which he said: "I accept the whole of the divinely inspired books of the

---

Barsanuphius was not in reclusion, but that it was Abbot Seridos' invention, and that he answered the questions instead of Barsanuphius. Therefore the holy one wrote a letter to the unbelieving one, and came to him personally and washed his feet, as well as the other brothers' feet who were serving there at that time. In this way that unbelieving brother believed, and all praised God (see Answer 60).

4. That is, by way of anathematizing him (editor's note).

Old and New Testaments, also the lives and divine writings of all God-bearing Fathers, both teachers and ascetics. I say this for the evil-minded Pamphilus, who, having come from the East, slandered these Holy Fathers: namely, Mark, Isaiah, Barsanuphius, Dorotheus and Hesychius—not the Barsanuphius and Dorotheus who were of the same mind with the Acephalites and with the so-called Decacerates (the ten-horned ones) and were for this given over to anathema by the holy Sophronius in his book. For these ones were absolutely different from the above-mentioned, whom I, according to the tradition of the Fathers, accept, having inquired about this of the presiding Patriarch Tarasius and other worthy Eastern Fathers. Besides, the image of Barsanuphius is placed on the covering of the altar table of the Great Church (Hagia Sophia in Constantinople), together with the depiction of the Fathers Anthony, Ephraim, and others. As for the writings of the above-mentioned Fathers, I did not find even the minutest impiety, but on the contrary much spiritual benefit."

11. JOHN THE PROPHET

The other Elder, St. John, conducted the same type of life of silence as did Barsanuphius, and became vouchsafed the same gifts of the Spirit—especially the gifts of clairvoyance and prophecy. Therefore he is called "the Prophet." For this reason, the great Barsanuphius told one man, who had first asked the divine John and, receiving an answer from him, had asked the same question of Barsanuphius: "The God of Barsanuphius and John is the same" (Answer 220). Also, when some people asked him to tell them about the life of John, he answered thus: "Concerning the life of my son, who is of one mind with me, the blessed and humble novice, who in everything has denied all his will, even unto death—what can I tell you? The Lord said: 'He who has seen Me has seen the Father' (John 14:9); and concerning the disciple said: 'May he be like his teacher' (Matt. 10:25). 'He who has ears to hear, let him hear' (Matt. 13:9)'' (Answer 129).

With these words the Saint wanted to show that the divine John was in everything similar to his father and teacher, Barsanuphius. The same thing is apparent from another incident. When some asked the divine John concerning matters, he had the habit of sending the enquirers to the great Barsanuphius himself, so that he would give them the answer. John did that because of his humility. That is why a certain Christ-loving man once said of him: "Why are you laughing at us, Father John, sending us to ask the holy and great Elder Barsanuphius, when you have equal power of the Spirit with him?'' (Question 792).

Where Saint John was from and who his kin were we do not know. He lived in the first cell of the great Barsanuphius, which the latter built outside the Gaza monastery. There he spent eighteen years in silence, up to his very death (Answer 221). No one ever saw him smiling, or being disturbed, or receiving the Divine Mysteries without tears, as was testified about him by the Abbot of that monastery (Answer 568).

Saint John prophesied much and made clairvoyant observations about life and death (Answers 685, 786). Together with Elder Barsanuphius he healed a certain Christ-loving and pilgrim-loving man from illness (Answer 793). Also, thanks to the gift of clairvoyance, he chose for ordination precisely those who were worthy of it (Answer 811). Because of the rich gift of prophecy which was given to him from the Lord, he was called by many, as we have already said, John the Prophet. For this reason also St. Nicon, in two books containing the answers of this Father, wrote: "John the Prophet.''

12. THE REPOSE OF SAINT JOHN

The holy John also foreknew his own death, about which he said thus: "In the week of Abbot Seridos' death I will die also. . . . If Abba Seridos would have lived longer, then I also would have lived five more years. But since God concealed this from me and took him, I also will not live much longer" (Answer 221).

But since Abba Elian, then still young in years, had been tonsured and placed as the Abbot of that monastery, not knowing the monastic rules and how to govern the brothers, he implored the divine John: "At least give me two weeks as a gift, so that I can ask you about the monastery and how to govern it." For this reason the Elder, having pity on him and being moved by the Holy Spirit that lived in him, said: "All right, I will stay with you two weeks." And thus Abba Elian questioned him about everything concerning the governing of the coenobitic monastery. When the two weeks passed, the holy Father called the whole monastery brotherhood, and having greeted each brother separately, dismissed them to their cells. And so he, in peace and silence, gave over his spirit into the hands of God (Answer 221).

When St. John died, St. Barsanuphius became absolutely silent and no longer gave answers to anyone, as Abba Dorotheus says in the introduction to his second homily. When Barsanuphius became silent, then also this very Abba Dorotheus left that monastery and organized his own (independent) community.

13. HEAVENLY REJOICING

Such was, O beloved brethren, the life of the God-bearing Fathers Barsanuphius and John. Such were their supernatural and heavenly gifts, which they were worthy to receive from God, also receiving such a divine end. And now, having ascended to the heavens, they are enjoying the ultimate bliss—seeing God face to face, whom they loved upon the earth with their whole soul—and are being illumined by the unutterable light of the three-sunned Divinity. They have settled in Heaven, and about them I will use the words of the divine Barsanuphius himself: "And being in this state

ST. ABBA DOROTHEUS OF GAZA
Reposed c. 620
Commemorated June 5

A disciple of Sts. Barsanuphius and John. His writings constitute the
"ABC's of monasticism." (See his Life in *The Orthodox Word*, 1969, no. 26.)
16th-century fresco in the refectory of the Monastery of Lavra, Mt. Athos

they reached the measure above distraction and high-mindedness—having become wholly mind, wholly eye, wholly light,
wholly perfect, wholly gods. Having labored they became
magnified, glorified, enlightened, alive again, because they
died before to everything. They are now rejoicing and cause
joy to all; they are rejoicing over the undivided Trinity, and
give joy to the angelic powers." And so, let us also wish
for their state; let us follow their path. Let us acquire their
humbleness and patience in order to receive their inheritance.
Let us keep their unfailing love, so as to inherit unutterable
good things: "Eye hath not seen, nor ear heard, neither have
entered into the heart of man, the things which God hath
prepared for them that love Him (I Cor. 2:9)" (Answer 120).

14. A BOOK FILLED WITH GRACE

These divine Fathers have loved their neighbors from the
bottom of their souls. They were benefactors to them and
rendered them help, not only during their lives, but even
after their death, since they left for all brethren this holy
book, as a Patristic inheritance to their spiritual children
—so that they, diligently reading it, would receive from it
great benefit for ages and ages. This book contains in it
850 answers to various persons: archpastors, pastors, monks,
laymen, elders, young ones, the infirm, and the healthy.
Some of these answers were written by the other Elder, John,
while the larger part of the others were given by the great
Elder Barsanuphius himself, not according to his own will,
but according to the dictates of the Holy Spirit for the good
of the soul, as he himself says: "And all this I write to you
not because of my own will, but according to the dictates of
the Holy Spirit—for the correction and for the benefit of
the soul and the conscience of the inward man" (Answer
131).

When the great Barsanuphius began to give these answers
to the Abbot of the monastery, St. Seridos, then something
worthy of wonder followed. St. Barsanuphius, having sum-

St. Sabbas Monastery in Palestine, near Bethlehem. To this monastery, about 70 miles from where he lived, St. Barsanuphius would send spiritual counsels.

moned Seridos, his writer, ordered him to write an answer to St. John, monk of St. Sabbas Monastery. Seridos, not being able to keep in mind all the words which the Saint told him, was wondering in hesitation how he could write such a multitude of words. He expected the Elder to order him to bring ink and parchment so that, while listening, he could write it down word for word. St. Barsanuphius, according to the grace of clairvoyance given to him by the Holy Spirit, read the secret thought of Seridos. His face suddenly shone like fire, and he said to Seridos: "Go and write, and do not fear. Even if I were to tell you a numberless multitude of words with the intent of you writing them down, then know that the Holy Spirit will not allow you to write one word more or less than what was said—even if you yourself would wish to, for He will direct your hand how to write it in the proper order" (Answer 1).

In such a way this book was written by the commandment of the Holy Spirit. From this alone anyone can understand how soul-profiting and good it is, how it is filled with the grace of spiritual discernment. For as the tree is, so is its fruit. Truly, any one can understand this from his own experience; for when he will begin reading this book, he will hear the words—uncomplicated and simple. And at the same time, secretly within his own heart, he will feel wondrous grace and the sweetness of the Holy Spirit, which like a magnet actively draws the will to oneness with God's will, and he will feel undoubting conviction in the truth of the words he reads. He will understand how all these words were brought out of an enlightened and God-bearing mind; how they issued from one heart, in which dwelt Jesus Christ and the Holy Spirit of Christ; and how they (these words) came from one soul which was all filled with peace and silence, was all Christ-like, all inspired by the fine wafting of a peace-giving and enlightening Spirit. And then he will know that, according to the words of David, "God hath spoken in His sanctuary" (Ps. 59:8), and that over the words of this book were fulfilled the promise of the Lord: "For you will not speak, but the Spirit of your Father will speak in you" (Matt. 10:20).

15. A RARE SOURCE OF PATRISTIC WISDOM

Thus accept, O beloved brethren, this soul-profiting book with joy and ardor. Read it diligently, for it is very profitable for bishops and priests, those in authority and judges, and especially monks—both those in silence and coenobium, those in the initial state, middle and perfect, especially for the infirm, those who find themselves in various sufferings and therefore have need of spiritual consolation. For this book, abundant in spiritual discernment, solves the most complicated questions. It is the teacher of patience: it is a hatchet that cuts off man-pleasing. It is a guide to true and perfect humility that instructs us to consider ourselves as nothing. It is the evangelizer of repentance, the birth-giver of weeping, and the provider of salvation of souls and perfection in Christ. For this reason the ancient divine Fathers would diligently study it; and many of its answers were incorporated into their own writings. Thus the holy Paul of Evergenitos put much of it into his book. Likewise, St. Nicon, who labored on the Black Mountain in Antioch in 1060, during the reign of Constantine Dukas and Patriarch John of Antioch, put much of the testimonies from it into two parts of his Anthology. St. Theodore the Studite, in his testaments, said that in this book of Barsanuphius he found nothing that was useless and disharmonious. And also St. Symeon the New Theologion, Peter Damascene and other Fathers mention this book. Accept it with joy also because, according to the general expression: "Everything rare is precious." This book is so rare that not only was it never printed, but even its manuscript is rarely to be found anywhere. According to the great mercy of God, only one complete and quite ancient manuscript copy of it appeared in the rich library of the Great Lavra of our holy and God-bearing Father, Athanasius of Mount Athos.

Who were the publishers of this book? The holiest of monks, Kyr Ananias, and the holiest of hieromonks, Cyprian and Euthymius—Athonites, the carvers of crosses. It was they who, having warm reverence for the holy and God-bearing Fathers Barsanuphius and John, and great love for this sacred book as the one that taught them various divine virtues (especially that of obedience—the noble cutting off of one's own will, and highly creative humility), copied it and moved me, their brother in spirit, to correct the copy and add to it the Life of the holy authors and a table of contents. But, depriving themselves of the crumbs of their

ST. NICODEMUS OF THE HOLY MOUNTAIN (MT. ATHOS)
1749-1809
Commemorated July 14

(See his Life in *The Orthodox Word*, 1965, no. 5.)

daily bread, they managed to publish only a few copies of this book, because they did not have the means to print many.

Therefore, read this book diligently, and become vouch-safed the grace-giving gifts which are locked in it. Draw from it everflowing benefit. Pray to God, O Christian brothers, concerning the soul-salvation of those who publish it to the glory of God, in honor of the Holy Fathers, and for your benefit.

Devoted to your love,
the least of monks
Nicodemus of the Holy Mountain
1803, June 22

STS. BARSANUPHIUS AND JOHN

Icon by Thomas Drain.

Guidance Toward Spiritual Life

by
SAINTS BARSANUPHIUS AND JOHN

13.

Longsuffering is the mother of all goods. Look at Moses, who chose for himself "rather to suffer with the people of God than to have the pleasure of sin for a time" (Heb. 11:25).

16.

Know, my brother, that if someone offends another either in deed or word, later he himself will be offended a hundredfold more.

17.

First I will accuse you: you call yourself a sinner, but in fact you do not show that you acknowledge this. One who acknowledges himself to be a sinner and guilty of many evils never contradicts anyone, does not quarrel with anyone, does not become angry at anyone, but considers everyone as better and more intelligent than himself. And if your thoughts, reviling you, tell you that this is so in actual fact—then how can they arouse your heart against those who are better than you? Be heedful, O brother—this is wrong. We have not yet attained to the point of considering ourselves sinners. He who loves the one who accuses him is most wise (Prov. 9:8). But if one loves someone and does not fulfill what he hears from him, this is more like hatred. If you are sinful, then why do you reproach your neighbor and accuse him, as though sorrow were coming to you through him? Do you not know that everyone is tested by his own conscience (Rom. 14:22), and this gives rise to sorrow in him. . . . And with regard to the fact that you consider yourself a fool (I tell you): Beware, lest you be deceived; test yourself, and you will find that you in fact do not consider yourself such; for if you think thus of yourself, you should not become angry at anyone, being in no condition to judge whether a matter has been done well or ill; after all, a fool is called senseless, and a fool and senseless one, as has been said, does not have in himself the salt (of wisdom), and not having salt in himself, how can he season and salt others? Behold, O brother, how we are made a mockery: we only speak with the lips, but in deeds we show something entirely different.

18.

Concerning warmth and coldness I will say: It is known that the Lord called Himself fire (Deut. 4:24, Heb. 12:29), which warms and kindles the heart and inward parts (Ps. 25:2). If this is so, then the devil, on the contrary, is cold, and from him comes every kind of coldness. If it were otherwise, then why was it said: "Then the love of many shall grow cold" (Matt. 24:10, 12)? What does "then" mean if it is not the time of the predominance of the adversary? If we feel coldness, let us call upon God, and He will come and warm our hearts with His perfect love not only for Him, but also for our neighbor, and from the face of His warmth the coldness of the hater of good will be banished.

21.

You know, O brother, that if one does not endure vexations, he will not behold glory either; and if he is not cleansed of gall, he will not experience sweetness. You have entered into the midst of the brethren and into the midst of various incidents in order to be heated and tested; and gold is not tested in any other way than by fire. . . .

Know, my brother, that every thought which is not preceded by the calmness of humility does not come from God, but clearly from the left side. Our Lord comes with quietness; but everything from the enemy comes with disturbance and unquietness. Although the demons also show themselves clothed in sheepskins, nonetheless, being rapacious wolves within, they are revealed by means of the disturbance which they cause.

35.

When we pray and God delays in hearing (our prayer), He does this for our benefit, so as to teach us longsuffering; wherefore we need not become downcast, saying: "We prayed, and were not heard." God knows what is profitable for a man. Rejoice in the Lord, leave off all your cares, and pray for me, O my beloved brother, one in spirit (with me).

37.

Q: Forgive me; like one who is drunk, I do not know what I am doing.

A: Examine what you have said: you do not know what you are doing. One who is drunk suffers from others: dishonor, blows, disdain, does not consider himself anything, does not show off his knowledge, does not teach others, does not give advice about anything, does not judge that this is good and that is bad. And if you speak one thing with the mouth and show something else in deeds, this means that you are speaking foolishly. Beware, lest your ears be suddenly struck by this: "Behold the Bridegroom, go out to meet Him" (Matt. 25:6, 10).

44.

A part of the bread which was sent to him as a blessing (from the Elder) Abba John gave to the one who served him, but not from his own hand (as he was not in the clergy), but he simply put it in a place and the other took it himself; and a second and a third time, receiving a blessing, (Abba John) did likewise; but doing this without the counsel (of the Elder), he did not understand that he was sinning in this.

The Elder wrote him that to place the blessed bread before the brother who was serving him and make him take it himself was not a deed of humility, but rather a deed of self-conceit and childish reason.

Once, when (Abba John), by the Elder's prayers, had received relief from passions, he said: "The passions have grown weaker in me." After this he sent (the Elder) a question about blasphemous thoughts and did not receive an answer. When he was surprised at the reason for this, suddenly, by God's allowance, to bring him to his senses, a frightful apparition was manifested to him, and it was repeated again, and then suddenly vanished.

(The Elder wrote to him concerning this:) You presumed to open your mouth before God and say that the passions have grown weaker in you, rather than to say: "They are all within me as in a storehouse"; and for this you were abandoned [by God], and all your wretchedness was uncovered.

47.

Do you desire to be delivered from sorrows and not to be weighed down by them?—Expect greater ones, and you will find peace. Remember Job and the other saints, what sorrows they endured; acquire their patience, and your spirit will be consoled. Be manful, be strong, and pray for me, remembering my words, and my soul will be renewed.

57.

O dearly beloved brother, one in soul (with me)! I inform you in the Lord that, seeing your sorrow and disturbance from the temptation which has come upon you, I have become pained in heart as never before—especially remembering the words of the Apostle: "Who is weak, and I am not weak? Who is scandalized, and I am not on fire?" (II Cor. 11:29). And again: "If one member suffer anything, all the members suffer with it" (I Cor. 12:26). And even if I do not act according to the Apostle, nonetheless I have heard that the Apostle has commanded to "Rejoice with them that rejoice, and weep with them that weep" (Rom. 12:15). Glory be to God on high, Who has not permitted the hater of good, the enemy, to pour out upon you all his malice as he would wish; for he would like to swallow men up alive, as the chief Apostle Peter testifies, saying: "As a roaring lion he goeth about, seeking whom he may devour" (I Peter 5:8). My Master! Let us not accept so readily disturbance from evil thoughts, so as to rise up and be disturbed against our brother: this comes only from the activity of the devil. What has become of "Blessed is the man that endureth temptation, for he hath been proved" (James 1:12) and the rest? I have written this to your love, not as to one who needs instruction, because if you enter into the Scriptures you will understand and will watch over yourself more than I; for I am wretched and infirm, and in vain do I bear just the name. But I have written to you with many tears, from pain of heart and a powerful love according to God.

58.

I am not ashamed to say to you, my brother, that you are not able to judge concerning the faith; and even if you are able to, do not do so; for by this you bring upon yourself only sorrow and disturbance. One who is firm in faith, if he will speak and contend with heretics or unbelievers, will never be disturbed, because he has within himself Jesus, the Source of peace and stillness. And such a one, after contending peacefully, can with love bring many heretics and unbelievers to the knowledge of our Savior Jesus Christ. Wherefore, O brother, since the judging of other subjects is above your measure, then keep to the royal path, I say, the faith of the 318 Holy Fathers [of the First Ecumenical Council] in which you were baptized: it includes within itself precisely everything for those who understand completely. . . . From now on do not be concerned over subjects which are not assigned to you, for the Lord has taken all cares away from you. . . . Pray for me, O brother, that it may not be said of me: "Thou that teachest another, teachest thou not thyself?" (Rom. 2:21).

59.

And now listen, my son, how to discern the thoughts of which you asked. When a thought suggests to you to do something according to the will of God, and you find in this matter joy, and at the same time sorrow which fights against it,—know that this thought is from God and compel yourself to endure, according to the word of the Apostle: "I chastise my body, and bring it into subjection: lest perhaps, when I have preached to others, I myself should become a castaway" (I Cor. 9:27), and fulfill the will of God.

But if there comes to you a thought from nature, that is, a natural desire, examine it diligently, and you will be in a condition to judge concerning it; for the Divine Scripture says: "Wherefore a man leaves his father and mother and cleaves to his wife, and the two will be one flesh" (Gen. 2:24). The Apostle, knowing that the will of God consists of abandoning not only what is demonic, but also what is natural, said: "The flesh profiteth nothing" (John 6:64). But he who cleaves to a wife is flesh, while he who cleaves to God is spirit (I Cor. 6:16, 17). Wherefore, they who desire to be spiritual must renounce the flesh: for what is not profitable is harmful; and what is harmful one must renounce. For those who desire to live devoutly in the world, the Apostle has said, "Marriage is honorable" (Heb. 13:4), and the rest.

As for thoughts which come from the demons, first of all, they are filled with disturbance and sadness, and they draw one after them secretly and subtly; for the enemies clothe themselves in sheepskins, that is, they instil thoughts which in appearance are right, but within are "ravening wolves" (Matt. 7:15), that is, they enrapture and "seduce the hearts of the innocent" (Rom. 16:18) by what seems to be good, but in actual fact is harmful. The Scripture says concerning the serpent that he is most wise; wherefore, observe always his head (Gen. 3:1, 15), lest he find openings in you and, settling in them, lay you waste. . . .

And so, if when you hear, think, or see anything, and your heart is even in the least disturbed, this is from the devil.

But if you have not attained the spiritual measure, but are still a child in mind, then humble yourself before your teacher, that "he may chastise you with mercy" (Ps. 140:5), and do nothing without counsel (Sirach 32:21), even though it might seem to you to be apparently good, for the light of the demons turns later into darkness.

62.

(Commentary) By the content of this reply the God-bearing Father quite clearly has shown that one who is concerned for his salvation should by no means ask questions in order to obtain knowledge only, for "knowledge puffeth up" (I Cor. 8:1), as the Apostle says. But to ask concerning the passions, and concerning how one should pass his life, that is, how to be saved, is most fitting; for this is necessary and leads one to humility. And humility is a shortened path to salvation, for it has been said: "I was humbled and the Lord saved me"

(Ps. 114:6). Likewise, one of the Saints says: "A humble-minded monk is not curious to know mysteries, but the proud one pries into God's judgments" (St. John of the Ladder, 25:11).

79.

Perfect humility of wisdom consists of bearing reproaches and dishonor and the rest which our Teacher Jesus suffered. . . . A sign of the fact that a man has touched on perfect prayer is the fact that he is no longer disturbed, even though the whole world might offend him.

81.

Concerning the measure of continence in food and drink the Fathers say that one should use both the one and the other a little less than necessary, that is, one should not fill the stomach completely. And everyone should determine for himself his measure both of cooked food and of wine. During wintertime no one drinks much; however, even then one should drink a little less than necessary, and he should act likewise with regard to food. In addition, the measure of continence is not limited only to food and drink, but extends also to conversations, to sleep, to clothing, and to all the feelings; in all of this there should be a measure of continence.

82.

During a time of disturbance and warfare of thoughts, one should lessen a little even the ordinary quantity of food and drink.

84.

To act "according to one's strength" means to use a little less than necessary both of food, and drink, and sleep. . . . As for food, restrain yourself when you wish to eat a little more, and in this way you will always make use of it moderately.

89.

Q: From whence comes the arousal of the body (i.e., fleshly warfare)?

A: Arousal of the body comes from negligence: negligence secretly draws you into judging and condemning (others), and through this it betrays you. When Israel truly served God, God preserved it from enemies; but when it became negligent in true service, God allowed its enemies to defeat it.

90.

Q: Should one ask the Elders concerning all thoughts which are born in the heart?

A: Brother! One should not ask (the Elders) concerning all the thoughts which arise, for some are momentary; but rather concerning those that remain a long time in a man and engage him in warfare. This matter resembles the case when a man, although he is vexed by many, disdains the enemies and is not concerned about them; but if someone (even a single one) will arise and attack him, he informs the leader concerning him.

104.

Q: Why does it happen to me that after I ask a question (of the Fathers) I judge another?

A: Judgment of another after asking a question happens to you because self-justification has not yet died in you: judge yourself, and you will cease to judge others.

109.

O beloved brother! The Lord endured the Cross, and you do not rejoice in sorrows, the endurance of which leads to the Kingdom of Heaven? It is a good sign that you sorrow; do you not know that when someone asks the Fathers to pray for him, or entreats God to give him help, that then sorrows and temptations are multiplied in order to test him?

And so, do not seek bodily repose if the Lord does not send it to you, for bodily repose is vile before the Lord, and the Lord said: "In the world you will have sorrow" (John 16:33). May God help you in everything. Pray for me.

124.

Q: My Father! How can I know, remaining in my cell, if I am cutting off my will? And what is the fleshly will, and what the will inspired by the demons, covered by a mask of goodness?

A: To cut off one's will while remaining in one's cell means not to take care for bodily repose in all its forms. The fleshly will consists of giving repose to the body in any circumstance, and therefore, if you do not give repose to it while you are in your cell, know that you are cutting off your will. . . . The will inspired by the demons consists of justifying oneself and believing oneself, and then a man is caught by them.

132.

Brother! Every repose of body is vile before our God; for He Himself said: "Narrow and strait is the way that leadeth into life" (Matt. 7:14). To choose this way is the good will [about which you ask], and he who holds to it in everything voluntarily chooses for himself sorrow according to his strength. . . . He who has the good desire of salvation, to every activity which is dictated by necessity, mixes in a small sorrow. For example: I can lie down to sleep on a soft bed stuffed with down, but I prefer a small sorrow (if it is really sorrow), and at my own desire I lie down on a mat for bodily repose, being ashamed of even this, because others repose on the bare ground, and some on pillows stuffed with husks, such as St. Arsenius and many others. And some also placed briars under their head, preferring sorrow.

And again: whether I find water near at hand, or what is useful in the kitchen—in working, I should choose the one that is farthest away, so as to bring the body a small sorrow. Again: can I have good food and pure bread?—I should prefer what is worse, so as to sorrow at least a little, remembering those who are suffering from hunger and do not eat cooked food at all, and all the more our Master Jesus, Who tasted gall and vinegar for my sake. This is the will according to God.

As for the fleshly will, it consists in the opposite of this, that is, to have repose in everything. Or do you not remember what we say every day?—"Close the door quickly, so we won't be bothered by the wind or by dust." And again: "Look here, brother, the food has burned and I can't eat it," and so forth. And to speak simply—in everything we act thus, and this is the evil will; cut it off, and you will be saved. And if you are conquered in this, reproach yourself, and justify your neighbor. O slothful brother! It is difficult to be saved! And how far one goes astray if he thinks to save himself by giving himself repose in everything! . . . Those only receive the Kingdom of Heaven who force themselves (Matt. 11:12). If we do not force ourselves a little, how can we be saved?

133.

It is not good to give oneself repose in everything. He who seeks this lives for himself, and not for God; for such a man cannot cut off his own will.

134.

When anyone is idle, he becomes occupied with the thoughts that come to him. But when he is occupied with work, he has no time to accept them. And so, from early morning keep your millstone (i.e., mind) within your power, and you will mill your wheat into bread for food. But if your adversary shall forestall you, then instead of wheat you will mill with it (the millstone) tares. . . .

If one takes a board on which something has been painted ahead of time, it will receive neither any new faces nor colors. And so, to be delivered of thoughts means to depict ahead of time on your board whatever is fitting. Let us labor according to our strength, and God will help us.

141.

If you are slandered—rejoice: this is very profitable for you. If you are offended, endure: for "he that endureth to the end, will be saved" (Matt. 10:22). For everything give thanks to God; because thanksgiving intercedes before God for human weakness. Always and in everything condemn yourself as one who sins and is deceived, and God will not condemn you; humble yourself in everything, and you will receive grace from God. If you will become accustomed to this, God will help you to obtain strength: for His will consists in this, that every man should be saved and come to the knowledge of the truth (I Tim. 2:4).

142.

Brother! Do not allow yourself to judge concerning the thoughts that come to you: this is a matter beyond your means; you do not understand their cunning, and that is why they disturb you just as they wish. But when they disturb you, say to them: "I do not know who you are; may God, Who knows this, not allow you to deceive me." And lay down before God your weakness, saying: "O Lord! I am in Thy hands; help me and deliver me from their hands." Any thought that tarries in you and engages you in warfare, reveal to your Abba, and he, with God's help, will heal you.

152.

He who smells the smell of his own foul odor does not smell the foul odor of anyone else, even though he might stand upon the breasts of corpses [the words of St. Sincletica]; and one who has been robbed by thieves has nothing to give others. Beware, O beloved: we who dwell outside of every concern and care do not even wish to consider that in actual fact we are earth and dust; and we have grown old, nourishing in ourselves vainglory. For to think that what we do is pleasing to God, that our dwelling in silence instructs others, and that we have been delivered from judgments and condemnations: all this is extreme vainglory and nothing else.

153.

If, according to the example of Abraham and Job, we think that we are earth and ashes (Gen. 18:27; Job 42:6), then we shall never be robbed, but we will always have something to give to others: not gold and silver, but an example of humility, patience, and love toward God. May there be glory to Him forever. Amen.

155.

The fact that my words remained fruitless is not your fault but mine: they are not the fruit of labors of sweat, wherefore they have no power.

156.

Blessed is he who has been purified of anger and the other passions, has kept all the commandments, and says: "I am a worthless servant" (Luke 17:10).

157.

Brother! The Divine Scripture says: "Do everything with counsel," and "without counsel do nothing" (Sirach 32:21). When you acted not according to counsel, but according to your own will, you labored foolishly; for there is no one who does not have need of someone to counsel him, except for Him Who created wisdom. But when you resolved to cut off your own will according to God, to enter into humility and accept the least of your brothers as an advisor, you thereby aroused to envy the enemy of good, the demon, who ever nourishes envy toward everyone. Do you see the stubbornness of the enemy? . . . Be heedful, and you will genuinely see that just as soon as you place a beginning, the enemy immediately presents to you a good-seeming pretext, and you destroy what you have begun. Then again you make a beginning, and again all the sooner destroy it. And you do not remember that "he that endureth to the end will be saved" (Mark 13:13), and "he who hath begun a good work in you will perfect it unto the day of Christ Jesus" (Phil. 1:6). If you act not according to your own will, as you have acted up to now, it will be easy for you, and I do not grieve over this; for I do not want to be anyone's abba or teacher, remembering the accusation of the Apostle: "Thou that teachest another, teachest thou not thyself?" (Rom. 2:21). Brother! The work of those being saved is to make the soul as refined as a spider web. And so, one needs much patience until through many sorrows we enter into the Kingdom of God (Acts 14:22) in Christ Jesus our Lord. Amen. Forgive me, brother, and pray for me.

160.

Let us always accuse ourselves: for victory consists precisely of this. As for the resolve to go away into the desert, as the Fathers said, there are three conditions, which if anyone observes, he can live both among people and in the deserts, and wherever he might go, namely: to reproach oneself, to leave one's own will behind him, and to consider oneself lower than all creatures. And let it be known to your love, that all the efforts of the devil are directed towards separating us from each other; for he clearly sees that the word of Scripture is fulfilled upon us: "brother being helped by brother, as a city firm and well-defended" (Prov. 18:19). May the Lord not permit him to fulfill his will in us, but may He crush him, according to the unlying word of Scripture, "swiftly under our feet" (Rom. 16:20).

161.

In all cases let us hasten to humility; for the humble one lies on the ground, and where can one fall who lies on the ground? But it is evident that one who is in a high place easily falls.

165.

The Scripture says: "We have passed through fire and water, and Thou hast led us out into repose" (Ps. 65:12); and those who desire to please God must go through small sorrows. How is it that we glorify the holy martyrs for the sufferings which they endured for the sake of God, if we ourselves cannot endure even a little sickness (fever)? Tell your sorrowing soul: "Is not a fever better for you than gehenna?". . . Know that they who want repose in everything will one day hear: "Thou didst receive good things in thy lifetime" (Luke 16:25) [Abraham's words to the rich man in hell]. Let us not weaken; we have a merciful God, Who knows our infirmity also better than us. If He, for the sake of testing, allows a disease to come upon us, we have treatment from the Apostle, who says: "God is faithful, Who will not suffer you to be tempted above that which you are able, but will with the temptation also make a way to escape, that ye may be able to bear it" (I Cor. 10:13).

168.

Who can depict, or who can search out the unutterable joy of the Saints, their unspeakable rejoicing and incomparable light; how the Lord reveals to them here the manifestation of His wondrous and most glorious mysteries and the glory and repose prepared for them; how He removes their mind from the present world, and they ever see themselves in heaven with Christ and His angels. Neither hunger, nor thirst, nor anything earthly causes them sorrow; for they have found freedom from the reproaches, passions, and sins of life, and in a word I shall say with the words of the Scripture: "Where their treasure is, there is their heart also" (Matt. 6:21).

169.

[To a sick monk] : Concerning fasting, do not grieve, as I have said to you before: God does not demand of anyone labors beyond his strength. And indeed, what is fasting if not a punishment of the body in order to humble a healthy body and make it infirm for passions, according to the word of the Apostle: "When I am weak, then am I strong" (II Cor. 12:10). And disease, more than this, is a punishment and takes the place of fasting and even more—for one who bears it with patience, thanks God, and through patience receives the fruit of his salvation; for instead of weakening his body by fasting, he is already sick without that. Give thanks to God that you have been delivered from the labor of fasting. Even if you will eat ten times in a day, do not grieve; you will not be judged for this, for you are doing this not at the demon's instigation, and not from the weakening of your thought; but rather, this occurs to us for our testing and for profit to the soul.

183.

For a beginner the following is appropriate: to remain in profound humility, in no case whatever to consider oneself to be something, not to say: "What is this, or what is this for?" But rather, one must remain in obedience and great submission, not to compare oneself with anyone, not to say: "Such a one is respected, why am not I respected? He has everything easy, and why do I not have ease?" To be disdained in everything and not become indignant—behold the works of a true beginner who really desires to be saved.

187.

Whether you are righteous or a sinner, in any case you must endure reproaches; for we cannot do without sorrow. Sorrow teaches us patience, and the Apostle, as a surpassing teacher of this, says: "Be . . . patient in sorrow (tribulation)" (Rom. 12:12); for sorrow stands before them who desire to be

62

saved. The Lord Himself has said: "In the world you will have sorrow" (John 16:33). And again it has been said: "Through many sorrows (tribulations) we must enter into the Kingdom of God" (Acts 14:22). Know, O brother, that He Who said: "My soul is sorrowful even unto death" (Matt. 26:38), desiring to save you, has allowed you to sorrow a little, so that for patience you might receive from Him mercy, there, at that terrible hour. If we wish to have repose in everything, then one day we will hear: "Thou didst receive good things in thy lifetime" (Luke 16:25). Our Master endured for us all sufferings: why then do not· we, remembering them, endure, so as to become communicants of them? We are given a commandment to give thanks for everything (I Thes. 5:18); and beware lest the hater of good draw us into ingratitude, and then we will lose everything.

188.

Your thought that "I came here to become the slave of men" is not yet humility. The Apostle boasted that he was the slave of everyone (I Cor. 9:19), and do you say this? When will you enter into this degree of humility? You do not know yourself, O brother, what you have said. May God forgive you.

(Commentary) Humility in words is the offspring of pride, and through it, it gives rise in disorderly fashion to its mother, vainglory, even though it might seem that what we have said is contrary to truth and does not correspond to the nature of things.

191.

Humility consists of considering oneself earth and ashes—in deed, and not in words only—and in saying: "Who am I? And who considers me to be something?"

193.

God leaves us to fall into arrogance and other passions so that we might acknowledge our infirmity and acknowledge where we are. In His goodness He leaves us, for our benefit, so that we might lay our trust and hope in Him, and not in ourselves. But beware of thinking that we fall into arrogance and other passions by God's will (for God's will is not in these); rather, God allows this to happen to us because of our negligence, and out of His love of mankind He brings us from our evil deeds to humility, for our own salvation.

195.

Without heedful ascetic labor there is no deliverance from temptation. And that the thought has come to you to go away from here is also a temptation, which comes from the devil's envy, through self-justification, so that you might be separated from the love of the Saints who pray for you and be deprived of their help.

196.

To the Monk Andrew, when he became faint from the temptations that had come upon him:

Andrew! My brother one in soul (with me), do not grow faint. God has not abandoned you and will not abandon you. But know that the sentence pronounced by the Master to our common father Adam: "In the sweat of your brow you shall earn your bread" (Gen. 3:19) is immutable. And just as this commandment is given to the outward man, so to the inward man it is commanded to aid the prayers of the Saints by means of one's own ascetic labors; and these prayers greatly help a man so that he will not remain fruitless. For just as gold which is heated in a furnace, held with pincers and beaten with a hammer, becomes pure and fit for a royal crown, so also a man being supported by the mighty and much-performing prayer of the Saints is heated by sorrows, receives the blows of temptations and, if he endures everything with gratitude, becomes a son of the Kingdom. And therefore, everything that might happen to you occurs for your benefit, so that you also might receive boldness before God, both through the intercession of the Saints and through your own labors. And do not be ashamed to offer now to God the beginning of these labors, lest in place of spiritual joy, sorrow should overtake you; and believe that He who has given the promises will fulfill them (Heb. 10:23). Prosper in the Lord, my beloved.

197.

To the same brother, when he had fallen into great dejection.

The Lord will not leave your labor fruitless. He has allowed you to suffer a little affliction so that you might not be a stranger to the Saints when you see them in that hour (of the Judgment) bearing the fruits of the endurance of tribulations and being glorified, so that you too might be a companion of them and Jesus, having boldness with the Saints before Him. Do not be sad, God has not forgotten you but is concerned for you as for His true Son, and not as for an adulterer. You labor well when you pay careful heed to yourself so as not to fall away from the fear of God and from thanksgiving to Him.

200.

God, who wishes to fulfill the word of Scripture in us also: "brother being helped by brother, as a city firm and defended" (Prov. 18:19), has brought your love to our infirmity, so that we might give help to each other for the sake of God. May our great Brother give help to us all; I mean our Lord Jesus. He has deigned to make us His brothers (Heb. 2:11); and we have already become such, and the Angels glorify us. O! Whom do we have for our Brother!

203.

And so, brother, hate perfectly so as to love perfectly. Depart completely, so as to draw near completely. Disdain one kind of adoption, in order to receive another adoption. Cease to fulfill desires, and you will fulfill desire. Wound yourself, and treat yourself. Mortify yourself, and bring yourself to life. Forget yourself, and know yourself. And you will have the works of a monk.

223.

If you desire a testament from me unto salvation and for your life: acquire extreme *humility and obedience* in everything; for they are the uprooters of all passions and the sowers of every good thing. . . . There is no need to write to you separately concerning every passion, for I have assigned you the treatment for them in one word: The Lord saith, "I will come to dwell in the humble" (Isaiah 57:15). What, then? Do you think that any kind of evil from the enemy can come to dwell where the enemy sees the living Lord? Know that an evil-doer cannot appear in the place where is the judgment seat of the Rulers.

224.

Take heed, O brother, lest (your thoughts) deceive you into doing what is of little benefit, such as sleeping in a sitting position, or not having a pillow, which are the same thing as "mint, and anise, and cummin," and instigate you "to leave the weightier things of the law" (Matt. 23:23), that is, the putting out of anger, the drying up of irritability, and being submissive in everything. (The thoughts) sow this in you in order to bring your body into exhaustion, from which you will fall into infirmity, and against your will you will ask for a soft bed and various foods; but it is better to be satisfied with one pillow and repose on it with the fear of God.

229.

Q: How can one be saved in the present times?
A: In every time, if a man can cut off his own will in everything, and have a humble heart, and death always before his eyes—he can be saved, by God's grace; and wherever he might be, fear does not take possession of him, for such a one "forgetteth the things that are behind, and stretcheth forth

to those that are before" (Phil. 3:13). Act thus, and you will be saved by God without sorrow.

231.

Q: Pray that I might place a beginning (to salvation).

A: The beginning is humility and the fear of God. "The fear of God is the beginning of wisdom" (Prov. 1:7). And what is the beginning of wisdom, if it is not to remove oneself from everything hateful to God? And how does one remove oneself from this? Do nothing without questioning and counsel; likewise, say nothing unfitting, and at the same time acknowledge oneself to be senseless, unsalted, and degraded, and in general insignificant.

234.

Q: Forgive me, my Lord Abba, for the Lord's sake. I bring to my memory that the Fathers say: "Let us enter our cell and remember our sins"; but when I remember them, I do not have pain of heart over them. Likewise, many times I desire contrition, but it does not come. Tell me: What hinders it from coming?

A: Brother! You are mocking when you say: "I desire," and in actual fact do not desire, because you do not desire truly. For to enter into one's cell refers to the soul and means to examine it and remove our thought from every man, and then we will be broken in spirit and feel contrition. But what hinders you from entering into contrition is your own will; for if a man will not cut off his own will, he cannot acquire pain of heart. And what prevents you from cutting off your own will is unbelief, and unbelief proceeds from the fact that we desire human glory; but the Lord said: "How can you believe, who receive glory one from another, and the glory which is from God alone you do not seek?" (John 5:44). Many times I have forbidden water from entering your belly through your mouth, but you draw it in with the nose: I mean by this fierce self-justification, which leads a man down to hell. Wherefore also the evil demons revile you, and what is convenient becomes for you inconvenient. If you wish to ask questions of me, then either leave off your own will, self-justification and the pleasing of men, or else I will leave you; for if you will not labor to cut off your own will, even against the inclination of your heart, then what benefit will there be from your asking questions? I told you: give yourself a hundred *denarii* and I will give you ten thousand of my *talents*. Behold, your previous transgressions are already forgiven, and yet you strengthen yourself by the wisdom of self-justification to enter into worse ones. Leave off, brother; this path does not lead to good. Mother Sarah said: "If I shall desire to please all men, I must repent at their doors." And the Apostle says: "If I yet pleased men, I should not be the servant of Christ" (Gal. 1:10). If in truth you wish to weep over your sins, pay heed to yourself and die for every man. Brother! Without labor a man cannot be saved. Cut off these three things: will, self-justification, pleasing of men; and in truth contrition will come to you and God will protect you from every evil. Brother! I repeat: pay heed to yourself, rejoice when you are beaten, accursed, slandered, punished. Leave off the slyness of the serpent, but not his wisdom; keep the gentleness of the dove together with wisdom, and the Lord will help you. Behold the path of salvation. If this path is pleasing to you, go on it, and God will give you a hand of help. But if you do not desire this— you yourself will see what will come of it. Everyone has a free will and the power to act. If you leave it to another, you will be free of care, and the other will take your cares upon himself. Choose what you want.

240.

Q: I cannot bear calmly the fact that I have only one garment.

A: Brother! Forcing oneself in everything, and humility, lead one to advancement; for the Apostle speaks thus: "In all things we suffer tribulation, but are not distressed"

(II Cor. 4:8). And when we entrusted to the Abba our material possessions and did not keep anything in our own hands, God knows and is witness to the fact that we did not do anything for which the Abba should thank us, but rather we are obliged to thank him that he has taken our burden from us and thus delivered us from cares. And the Apostle Peter said: "Be ye subject to every human authority for God's sake" (I Peter 2:13), and James said: "And whosoever shall keep the whole law, but offend in one point, is become guilty of all" (James 2:10). Wherefore no one should have his own will, but one should rather reproach himself; through which a man also receives God's mercy. And if through the devil's mockery such a one imagines of himself that he has acted well, he loses everything that he has done. And therefore be humble-minded, acting as you did before, saying: "Forgive me, O Lord, that I have burdened the Abba, laying my burden upon him." May the Lord Jesus Christ save us. Amen.

241.

Q. Another brother, a deacon, refused to serve at the altar of preparation, remembering his previous sins, and he asked the Great Elder both regarding this and regarding his bodily infirmity.

A: Brother! The Scripture instructs us that "those who would live piously in Christ Jesus will be persecuted" (II Tim. 3:12). But from whom, in the present age, can one suffer persecution? From the demons, who push one away from the fear of God and from the service of God. Repentance for a sin demands that one do it no more, and withdrawal from evil consists of abandoning it. May your previous sins not cause you offense; and do not decline from the service of God with fear and trembling. Remember, that this (service) is the sanctification of your soul. If you will believe this, you will always pay heed to yourself with trembling, lest you sin and be deprived of this sanctification. And thus, endure sufferings and tribulations with thanksgiving; for this is God's chastisement, and God will have mercy on you and make them to be for the salvation of your soul. Amen.

242.

Q: Tell me, my Father, is irritability natural or unnatural, and what difference is there between these?

A: Brother! There is a natural irritability and there is an unnatural irritability. The natural one opposes the fulfillment of lustful desires, and it does not need treatment, being sound. The unnatural one rises up if lustful desires are *not* fulfilled. This latter one requires means of treatment which are more powerful than the desire. He who gives the warrior strength is greater than he [i.e., man than his passion], and if he ceases to give strength, the warrior [irritability], no longer finding strength, becomes inactive.

244.

Q: I suffer from my passions of soul: Tell me, for the Lord's sake, what I should do to be delivered from them.

A: Brother! He who desires to be saved and to become a son of God must acquire great humility, obedience, submission, and meekness. Behold: you asked what you should do. I told you this, and I vouch for it, that neither the enemy nor passion will take possession of you. For they are consumed by humility as by fire, and the heart finds repose, being enlightened in Christ, to Whom may there be glory. Amen.

245.

Q: How am I to know, my Father, whether I am living pleasing to God or receiving harm because I am not living together with the brethren in the coenobia, but apart [serving a certain Elder] . . . . And since impure passion troubles me a great deal, I ask: "What is the sign of agreement with [sinful] thoughts?"

A: (John) when you wish to know whether you receive benefit or harm living separately, find out by the following sign:

if you are living thus out of obedience, know that you are receiving benefit. For the Scripture says that "obedience is greater than sacrifice" (I Kings 15:22). But if you are contradicting [your Father], then you are harming yourself; for this is the evil will. . . .

Concerning vile and hateful passion, I will say: To uproot it, it is essential to have labor of heart and body: labor of heart, so that the heart might constantly pray to God; labor of body, so that a man might mortify and subject his body, according to his strength. Agreement with thoughts consists of this: when something pleases a man, he enjoys this in his heart and reflects on it with satisfaction. But if one contradicts the thought and wages warfare with it so as not to accept it: this is not agreement, but warfare, and this brings a man to experience and success. May the Lord Jesus Christ cleanse you from your sins and strengthen you by His grace in your infirmity. Amen.

The questions of Abba Dorotheus to the Great Elder:

252.

Q: I am being strongly attacked by sexual passion; I am afraid that I may fall into despondency, and that from the infirmity of my body I will not be able to restrain myself; pray for me, for the Lord's sake, and tell me, my Father, what I should do?

A: Brother! The devil, out of envy, has raised up warfare against you. Guard your eyes and do not eat until you are full. Take a little wine for the sake of the body's infirmity of which you speak. And acquire humility, which rends all the nets of the enemy. And I, who am nothing, will do what I can, entreating God that He might deliver you from every temptation and preserve you from every evil. Do not yield to the enemy, O brother, and do not give yourself over to despondency, for this is a great joy to the enemy. Pray without ceasing, saying: "Lord Jesus Christ, deliver me from shameful passions," and God will have mercy on you, and you will receive strength by the prayers of the Saints. Amen.

253.

Q: The same brother, being attacked by the same sexual passion, asked the same Great Elder to pray for him and to tell him how to distinguish whether a man is being tempted by his own lusts or by the enemy.

A: Brother! Without labor and contrition of heart no one can be delivered from passions and please God. When a man is tempted by his own lust, this may be known from the fact that he is careless about himself and allows his heart to reflect about what he has done before; and then a man himself draws passion unto himself through his own lust. His mind, being little by little blinded by passion, begins, unnoticeably for himself, to pay attention to someone for whom he feels attraction, or to speak with him, and he finds occasions on which to converse with him or to sit with him, and by all means he strives to fulfill his desire. If one allows thoughts to pay heed in this, warfare will increase until a fall, albeit not in body but in spirit, in agreement with thoughts; and it turns out that such a man lights the fire himself in his own substance. But a sober and prudent man who desires to be saved, when he sees from what it is that he suffers harm, carefully preserves himself from evil remembrances, is not drawn into passionate thoughts, avoids meetings and conversations with those for whom he feels attraction and avoids every occasion for sin, fearing lest he himself ignite a fire within himself. This is the warfare which proceeds from one's own lust, which a man brings on himself. . . .

Tame your steed with the bridle of knowledge, lest, looking here and there, he become inflamed with lust towards women and men and throw you, the horseman, to the ground. Pray to God, that He may turn "your eyes, lest they see vanity" (Ps. 118:37). And when you will acquire a manful heart, warfare will depart from you. Cleanse yourself, as wine cleanses wounds, and do not allow stench and filthiness to accumulate in you. Acquire weeping, so that it might remove from you freedom [looseness] in your relations, which destroys the souls that adopt it. Do not throw away the implement without which fertile land cannot be worked. This implement, made by the Great God, is humility: it uproots all the tares from the field of the Master and gives grace to those who dwell in it. Humility does not fall, but raises from a fall those who possess it. Love weeping with all your heart, for it also is a participant in this good work. Labor in everything to cut off your own will, for this is accounted to a man for sacrifice. This is what is meant by: "For Thee we are mortified all the day, we are accounted as sheep for slaughter" (Ps. 43:22). Do not weaken yourself by conversations, for they will not allow you to prosper in God. Firmly bridle the organs of your senses: sight, hearing, smelling, taste, and feeling, and you will prosper by the grace of Christ. Without tortures no one is a martyr, as the Lord also has said: "In your patience possess ye your souls" (Luke 21:19), and the Apostle says, "in much endurance, in sorrows" (II Cor. 6:4).

254.

Q: Having many sins, I wish to repent, but because of bodily infirmity I cannot labor like the Fathers; I beg you, tell me: how can I make a beginning?

A: Brother! They are poor whom the Lord glorifies because they have renounced all their possessions, that is, all their passions, and have become stripped of them for the sake of His Name, such ones are poor in truth, and to them belongs blessedness. And there are other poor who have acquired nothing good, whom the Lord threatens, saying: "Depart from Me, ye cursed" (Matt. 25:41). He who has such possessions and is burdened by them, let him renounce them, so that he may remain without care. And so, if you desire to make a beginning of repentance, look at what the harlot did: with her tears she washed the feet of the Master (Luke 7:38).

Lamentation will wash anyone of sins; but a man attains lamentation with difficulty, by means of much instruction in the Scriptures, of patience, of reflection on the terrible Judgment and eternal shame, and through self-renunciation, as the Lord has said: "He who would come after Me, let him renounce himself and take up his cross and follow after Me" (Matt. 16:24). And to renounce oneself and take up one's cross means: to cut off one's own will in everything and consider oneself to be nothing. Since you have said that you are infirm in body and can do nothing—therefore, do according to your strength, taking bread and drink a little less than ordinarily, for God accepted the two mites of the widow and rejoiced over them more than over all the rest. Instruct yourself not to be free in your relations with others, and you will be saved.

255.

Q: Pray for me, my Father, I am very much disturbed by thoughts of sexual sin, despondency, and fear; and a thought says to me that I should converse with a brother to whom I feel attracted when I see him, lest by my silence I give him occasion for suspicion. I feel likewise that the demons are somehow pressing me, and I fall into fear.

A: Brother! You are not yet instructed in warfare with the enemy, which is why there come to you thoughts of fear, despondency, and sexual sin. Stand against them with a firm heart, for combatants, unless they labor, are not crowned, and warriors, unless they show the King their skill in battles, do not become worthy of honors. Remember what David was like. Do you not also sing: "Test me, O Lord, and try me, kindle my inward parts and my heart" (Ps. 25:2). And again: "If a regiment arm itself against me, my heart will not fear. If warfare shall rise up against me, I will hope in Him" (Ps. 26:3). Likewise, concerning fear: "For if I should go in the midst of the shadow of death, I will fear no evil, for Thou art with me" (Ps. 22:4). And concerning despondency: "If the spirit of the powerful one should come upon thee, do not leave thy place" (Eccl. 10:4).

Do you not wish to be skilled? But a man who is not tested by temptations is not skilled. It is battles that make a man skilled. The work of a monk consists of enduring battles and opposing them with manfulness of heart. But since you do not know the cunning traps of the enemy, he brings thoughts of fear and weakens your heart. You must know that God will not allow against you battles and temptations above your strength; the Apostle also teaches this, saying: "Faithful is the Lord, Who will not leave you to be tempted more than you can bear" (I Cor. 10:13).

Brother! I also in my youth was many times and powerfully tempted by the demon of sexual sin, and I labored against such thoughts, contradicting them and not agreeing with them, but presenting before my own eyes eternal tortures. For five years I acted thus every day, and God relieved me of these thoughts. This warfare is abolished by unceasing prayer with weeping.

And the fact that the demons are pressing you proceeds from their envy; if they could, they would chase you out of your cell also; but God does not allow them to take possession of you, for they do not have authority for this. God could swiftly relieve you, but then you would not begin to oppose another passion [when it comes]. May the demons not weaken you so as to turn your attention to a brother (to whom you are attracted), or to converse with him; but if you should happen unexpectedly to come together with him, against your desire, restrain your glance with fear and decency and do not listen attentively to his voice. And if this brother, out of ignorance, should himself begin to speak with you or sit next to you, then skillfully avoid him, but not suddenly, rather with decorum. Say to your thought: "Remember the terrible Judgment of God and the shame which will then overtake those who are attracted by these shameful passions." Compel your thought, and you will receive help, by the prayers of the Saints, and God will have mercy on you. Do not be a child in mind, "but a child in malice" (I Cor. 14:20); in mind, O brother, be perfect. Pay heed to yourself, as to how you will meet God. Amen.

256.

Q: Pray for me, my Father, for I am wretched in everything, and I have need of great love of mankind. The thoughts which arise in me say: "Go to a different place and there you will be saved." By your prayers, may God not allow me to be possessed by this thought.

A: Brother! May he be cursed who has sowed in your heart such thoughts of leaving this place because of the transgression of commandments [here]. This is the devil. He presents this to you under an appearance of truth, so that, having mocked you, he might make you an object of scandal for many, so that you might bear condemnation from them also. Besides, you are being subjected to this for your negligence and vainglory. You say: "If I go away to a different place, there I will endure dishonor." But why is it that now, just as soon as you hear that your brother has said something against you, your heart is disturbed, and you do not wish that anyone should know of your transgression? To negligence and vainglory the demons also join their nets so as to cause your soul to perish. Be assured in the Lord, that if it were not for the help of God and the prayers of the true slaves of God who are here, you could not remain even a year in the monastery. But just as a blind man sees nothing, so also you do not see the benefactions which God has shown you and continues to show by the prayers of the Saints and blessed Abraham, who said to you and your brother: "If you remain in this place, you will have me as an intercessor." Brother! Pay careful heed to yourself; labor against thoughts so as not to fall into negligence and vainglory, not to do anything according to your own will, and not to accept the thoughts of self-justification which arise in you: otherwise you will be subjected to a powerful fall. Know for sure, that wherever you might go, though you might go over the whole earth from end to end, nowhere will you receive such benefit as in this place. What an anchor is for a boat, such will be for you the prayers of the Fathers here. Acquire firmness, and it will remove from you familiarity in your relation with your near ones, which is the cause of all evils in a man. Leave off all outward care, and then you will freely serve God. Become dead to every man: in this consists being a stranger [on earth]. Consider yourself as nothing, and your thought will not be disturbed. Do not think that you have done anything good, and your reward will be preserved whole. Above this, remember that you will not remain long in the body, and strive so that you might be able to say with boldness in that hour: "I prepared myself and was not disturbed" (Ps. 118:60).

Brother! One cannot live without labor, and no one is crowned without struggling. Force yourself to struggle for your salvation, and God will help you, "Who wisheth that all men be saved and come to the knowledge of the truth" (I Tim. 2:4). May He have mercy on you, my son, so that with fervor you might enter upon pleasing Him. For His is the mercy and power and glory unto the ages of ages. Amen.

257.

Not all living in a monastery are monks, but only he is a monk who fulfills the work of a monk. The Lord said: "Not everyone who says to Me, Lord, Lord, will enter into the Kingdom of Heaven, but he who does the will of My Father Who is in Heaven" (Matt. 7:21). . . .

God allows you to be subjected to temptations during sleep, to the attack of the demon who presses you, so that you might come to understanding and reproach yourself, as befits a monk; but you do not understand this, brother. Time is given us that we might test our passions, weep and lament. But if you, remaining in your cell, are dispersed in your thoughts—then reproach yourself in everything and lay down your infirmity before God. He will help you and strengthen you to prosper in Him. Amen.

258.

If you wish to be delivered from shameful passions, do not behave with anyone familiarly, especially with those toward whom your heart is inclined by a lustful passion; through this you will be delivered also from vainglory. For in vainglory is involved the pleasing of men, in the pleasing of men is involved familiarity of behavior, and familiarity of behavior* is the mother of all passions.

261.

Q: My Father! You have shown mercy to me the infirm one and gave me advice, whenever I am doing or saying anything, to call upon the Name of God and your prayers, and you said that through this I would have success. I am forcing myself to do and speak in accordance with the will of God; but it happens that sometimes I forget (to call on the Name of God and your prayers) in my negligence, and therefore I entreat you: ask for me of God sobriety, and do not allow me to wander according to my own will. I also entreat you to tell me how I should act in the case when, having called on the Name of God and your prayers in some matter, I still doubt whether to do the matter or not. Likewise, if I am asked about something, and the one who asks immediately demands an answer, before I can manage to call on God or think what to say: how am I to act with regard to such an unexpected question?

A: If one receives from the Fathers a testament, a counsel or an answer concerning something, and out of forgetfulness or negligence forgets it,--then, acknowledging that he has sinned, let him repent, and God will forgive him. . . . If it should happen to you to do something, and you call on God and the prayers of the Saints, but still have doubts—then do this mat-

---

* The Slavonic term literally means "brazenness."

ter, it is in accordance with God's will, for at its beginning you called on God. As for what to answer to an unexpected question—there is nothing swifter than the mind; raise it up to God, and He will grant you what to reply without disturbance.

[Notice how the Father guides the disciple from seeking for *rules* of behavior up to trusting in God.]

262.

Without pain of heart no one receives the gift of discerning thoughts [the motives of actions and the like]. I shall entreat God to grant it to you, but let your heart also be pained a little, and God will grant you this gift. . . . When God, by the prayers of the Saints and for the pain of your own heart, will grant you this gift, you will then always be in a condition to discern thoughts by His Spirit.

263.

Q: Enlighten me, my Father, as to how my heart should labor so as to attain the gift of discernment.

A: The labor of your heart must consist of ceaselessly praying to God that He will not allow you to wander astray or follow your own desires: through this you will attain discernment.

264.

Every gift is received through pain of heart.

265.

And so do not grow faint, but as long as you have time, act, be humble, be obedient, submit, and God will help you, Who gives grace to the humble but opposes the proud (I Peter 5:5). Say without ceasing: "Jesus, help me," and He will help.

268.

Restrain your tongue from idle talking, your stomach from love of sweetness, and do not irritate your neighbor. Do not be brazen, consider yourself as nothing, preserve love toward everyone, and have always God in your heart, remembering, "when I shall appear before the face of God" (Ps. 41:3). Keep this, and your soil will bring forth a hundred-fold of fruit to God, to Whom may there be glory unto the ages. Amen.

269.

Q: My Father, what does it mean to consider oneself as nothing?

A: Brother! To consider oneself as nothing means not to compare oneself with anyone, and not to speak of one's own good deeds; I also have done this.

274.

He who unites humility with labor, soon attains [his aim]. He who has humility with abasement likewise attains, for abasement takes the place of labor. But he who has only humility, though he may also prosper, does so not as swiftly. He who desires to acquire true humility should in no case whatever consider himself to be anything. In this consists true humility. . . .

If you wish to be delivered from forgetfulness and captivity, you may attain this by no other way than by acquiring in yourself spiritual fire, for only from its warmth do forgetfulness and captivity disappear. And this fire is acquired by striving toward God. Brother! If your heart will not seek the Lord day and night with pain, you will not prosper.

275.

Humility consists in this: never, in any circumstance, to consider yourself to be something; to cut off your will in everything; to be subject to everyone; and to bear without disturbance everything that comes to you from outside. That is true humility in which there is no room for vainglory. One who has humility of wisdom should not strive to express his humility in words, but it is sufficient for him to say: "Forgive me," or "Pray for me." He likewise should not take upon himself to perform menial tasks, for both the one and the other lead to vainglory, hinder advancement [in spiritual life] and cause more harm than benefit. But when you are commanded to do something—not to talk back, but to do it with obedience: this is what leads to advancement.

Abasement is of two kinds: one is of the heart, and the other comes from offenses received from outside. The abasement that comes from outside is greater than that of the heart; for it is easier to abase oneself than to bear abasement from others, because the latter causes much greater pain in the heart.

281.

With regard to the tongue, familiarity, and gluttony, about which you have asked me to pray--strive yourself, according to your strength, to refrain [from them] , for one cannot restrain them without pain of heart, without sobriety and lamentation, remembering that "the prayer of a righteous man availeth much" (James 5:16). All the passions are conquered by humility, which everyone acquires only by labor.

282.

Lamentation does not proceed from tears, but tears from lamentation. If a man, being among others, cuts off his own will and pays no heed to the sins of others, he will acquire lamentation. For through this his thoughts are gathered together, and being gathered together in this way, they give birth in the heart to sorrow according to God (II Cor. 7:10), and this sorrow is—tears.

285.

Brother! He who wishes to be a monk must not have his own will in anything. Christ, in teaching us this, said: "I came into the world not to do My own will" (John 6:38), and the rest. For he who wishes to fulfill one thing and refuses to do something else, shows either that he is more discerning than the one who commands him, or else he is mocked by demons. And thus, you should obey in everything, even though it might seem to you that the matter will not be without fault. The Abba who assigns it to you will bear your sin also, for he will have to give answer for you. If the matter assigned seems difficult to you, ask the Abba about this and leave it to his judgment. If the brethren should assign you a similar work, and you see or know that it is harmful, or surpasses your strength, again ask the Abba, and do whatever he says.

286.

Q: When a brother asks me about some word or matter which I do not know, should I reply to him or not? Likewise, when I am not asked, but I myself see that someone is doing something badly, should I at least once speak about this to the one who is doing badly, or not?

A: To all these questions there is a single answer: be careful not to speak out of vainglory, but speak with humility and the fear of God. In all the cases (about which you ask), speak and remind [another], if necessary—but only in your own monastery, and not in a different place; because those who live in one community are as it were one body. But when you are in a different place, say nothing of yourself, so as not to show yourself a teacher; but when you are asked, speak with humility, and God will instruct you, O brother.

287.

To say something with humility does not mean to speak like a teacher, but rather, just as you have heard from the Abba and from the Fathers. If it is profitable to say something to a brother, and vainglory inspires you to enjoy this,—then know that the enemy wishes to hinder you from doing something of profit to your brother. If you will listen to vainglory, your brother will never receive profit through you. But over-throw vainglory and disdain it, and when you say what is nec-essary to your brother, repent before God, saying: "Forgive me, O Lord, that I spoke out of vainglory."

288.

Q: My Father! How to reconcile these two things: you com-manded me, when I see something unprofitable, to speak be-fore I am asked; but the Fathers say that one should not be-gin a conversation before being asked.

A: Brother! The Elders reply in accordance with the (spiri-tual) stature of a man. There is a time when a man can serve, and then he should give his service to others; but there also comes a time when others will serve him: then his spiritual stature will no longer be what it was before. To the perfect, what is perfect is said; but those who are under the law are given something else, for they are still being tested under a guide.

Q: Tell me, my Father, what it means to pay heed to one's thoughts? Should one be occupied with this at a definite time? And how does one do this?

A: The Fathers have assigned a time for paying heed to one's thoughts saying: "In the morning test yourself, how you spent the night; and in the evening likewise, how you spent the day. And in the middle of the day, when you are weighed down by thoughts, examine yourself."

290.

Q: When a brother does something neutral [neither good nor bad] but not in accordance with my will, and I am grieved over this, how should I act: be silent and not pacify my heart, or speak gently and thereby be delivered from distur-bance? And if this matter causes grief to others but not to me: should I speak for the sake of others; or will this be a futile interference in the business of another?

A: If the matter is without sin, neutral, and you wish to speak only so as to make your own heart calm, in this you reveal your conviction that you, because of your infirmity, cannot endure. Rather reproach yourself and be silent. But when a brother causes grief to others, tell your Abba, and he will either speak to this brother himself or instruct you what to say to him, and you will be calmed.

297.

Q: If I speak a sarcastic word to someone, and he doesn't understand it, should I repent before him, or be silent and give him no thought about this?

A: If the brother does not understand that you spoke to him in sarcasm, be silent and do not disturb him; but strive to repent over this before God.

301.

Q: If a passionate thought enters my heart, how should I repel it: by opposing it and pronouncing a prohibition and as it were becoming angry at it; or by hastening to God and laying my weakness before Him?

A: Brother! Passions are the same as sorrows, and the Lord did not distinguish them but said: "Call on Me in the day of thy sorrow, and I will deliver you, and you shall glorify Me" (Ps. 49:15). And therefore, with relation to any passion there is nothing more profitable than to call on the Name of God. To oppose (the thoughts) is fitting not for everyone, but only for those who are strong in God, to whom the demons are subject; but if one who is not strong will oppose, the demons will revile him, as someone who opposes them while being in their power. Likewise, to prohibit them is the work of great men who have power over them. Have many of the Saints prohibited the devil as did Michael the Archangel, who did this because he had the power? For us infirm ones it remains only to hasten to the Name of Jesus; for the passions, as has been said, are demons, and they depart (from the invocation of this Name). And what do you wish more than this? May God strengthen you in His fear and grant you the victory.

304.

Q: What shall I do? I fear the shame of dishonors. And if I enter into conversation with certain ones, I am very much drawn away by this and am captivated so that I completely forget myself; and when I remember myself, I am ashamed to leave those with whom I am conversing and go away.

A: So that an infirm one might not fall into all this and into love of glory, he should in every way flee from talkativeness and cut off conversation, excusing himself by means of the Abba, saying that supposedly he had commanded him to do something, and therefore he is in a hurry. And not to bear dishonor is a deed of unbelief. Brother! Jesus became a man and bore dishonor, and are you greater than Jesus?—This is unbelief and a demonic deception. He who desires humility, as he says, and does not bear dishonor, cannot attain humility. . . . Concerning shame, I say: Reflecting on the shame before everyone which will come upon sinners before the Lord, consider temporal shame to be nothing at all.

305.

Q: When visitors come to the monastery, either laymen or Fathers, a thought induces me to ask of them concerning the benefit of the soul or concerning some other matters. How do you judge concerning this?

A: Brother! He who truly desires to be a disciple of Christ has no authority over himself in anything, so as to do anything of himself. Even though he might think to obtain profit from conversation with visitors, still he violates the commandment which says: "Do all with counsel" (Sirach 32:24). And what do you want to hear above what the Fathers have said? If some of those who come will speak about the word of God, then ask your Abba with humility: "Abba, do you desire that I should wait and listen, or should I go?" And whatever he says, that do calmly. And if out of need you wish to ask something of someone, whether monk or layman—tell the Abba, and when he finds it needful he will himself ask what you need to know; and when he tells you: "Ask yourself"—then ask.

306.

Q: And if I do not wish to ask, but I happen to meet with a visitor, or someone himself asks me about something, how do you command that I act?

A: When meeting with someone, limit yourself to a greeting, and then say: "Pray for me, I am going on business"; and go. When they ask you about something and you know about this, speak and then leave; if you don't know, say: "I do not know"; and then leave.

307.

Q: If someone comes upon me when I am sitting or doing something and sits next to me and wishes to speak with me, what should I do?

A: If someone comes upon you sitting somewhere and comes up to you, take a blessing from him and do as said before, and say to him: "Pray for me." And even though he might restrain you with his hands, tell him: "Forgive me, I have been given the commandment not to speak with anyone without the permission of the Abba; but I will tell him, and whatever he commands I will do." If someone comes up to you and sits down while you are doing something—then, according to the commandment given you, find some pretext and stand up.

308.

A true disciple and one who desires to be a monk preserves himself from conversations (with visitors), for from them are born: carelessness, weakness, lack of submission, and extreme boldness.

309.

As to whether to cut off meetings with visitors all at once, or little by little, so visitors will not be surprised.

A: If you cut off the meeting all at once, you will be calm; otherwise you will give occasion (for new conversations and various thoughts). For conversations, because visitors will say: Previously he conversed with me, and so I will converse with him. And for thoughts—because someone will think: probably this brother has something against me, for previously he spoke with me and now he does not speak. Desire to attain this, and God will help you.

317.

He who conceals his thoughts remains unhealed, and he is corrected only by frequently asking the spiritual Fathers about them.

324.

Q: Since you have assigned me to be in this service, in the infirmary, tell me, my Father: should I read certain medical books and teach myself to make medicines, or is it better not to be concerned about this, as something that causes the mind to wander, and abandon it (so that it will not arouse vainglory in me) and be satisfied with what I already know, doing whatever is possible with the aid of oil, flour, ointments, and in general simple remedies such as are used by those who do not read (medical books). How should I act? For my heart trembles in this service lest I sin in something and add to my passions yet other sins.

A: Inasmuch as we have not yet come to perfection, so as to be entirely delivered from the captivity of passions, it is better to occupy ourselves with medicine than with passions. But we should place our hope not in medicines but in God, Who kills and brings to life and says: "I will strike and I will heal" (Deut. 32:39). While reading medical books or asking someone about them, do not forget that without God no one receives healing. And thus, he who devotes himself to the medical art should give himself over to the Name of God, and God will grant him help. The medical art does not hinder a man from being pious; but make use of it like a handiwork for the benefit of the brethren. Whatever you do, do with the fear of God, and you will be preserved by the prayers of the Saints. Amen.

325.

Q: You told me before that the cutting off of one's own will consists also of not arguing out of a desire to stand on one's own. But what should I do, my Father: sometimes it happens that I bring a sick man something that is apparently beneficial; but often it harms him, and I grieve that in this I have done my own will. I see likewise that I am occupied the whole day, and this somehow does not allow me to remember God. Also, gluttony disturbs me. Tell me, what should I do? For I believe that in these things is my salvation.

A: If, thinking that something will bring benefit to the sick, you act according to your will, and the opposite happens, that it brings them harm—God, who beholds your heart, will not judge you; for He knows that you have done harm while desiring to bring benefit. But if someone who knows (about this matter) should tell you about it beforehand, and you should disdainfully disobey him, this would be pride and self-will. Many have constantly heard about some city or other and then they chance to enter it without knowing that it is that very city; so you also, O brother, spend the whole day in remembrance of God and do not know it. To have a commandment and strive to keep it—this is submission to and remembrance of God. Brother John has rightly said to you: first put on leaves, and then, when God commands, you will bear fruit. If you do not know what is profitable, follow one who knows, and this is humility, and you will receive God's grace. You have rightly said that your salvation lies in this;

for you did not come here of yourself, but God guided you here. "Be strong in the Lord" (Eph. 6:10): you receive not a little benefit from the occupation about which you complain. As far as possible, struggle against gluttony. And the Lord will help you to know and do what is profitable. Be manful and strengthened in the Lord.

327.

Q: I am apprehensive, my Father, because I am in charge of the infirmary, for this is something involving authority, and this might give occasion for vainglory and familiarity. Likewise, from frequent eating of food I can be drawn into gluttony. And so, do you not consider that, for a preliminary training of myself, I should be first in a lower obedience, and then, when it will be easier for me, I should again enter upon that service?

A: Listen, O brother, and be convinced in the Lord, that when we entrusted this matter to you, our hand and our heart are with you, or to be more precise, the hand of God, entreated by our prayers for the salvation of your soul; and that He has strengthened you in this matter and given you success and covered you in it. You can be saved in no other way than through this (obedience). And so, do not become discouraged, falling and rising up, crawling and reproaching yourself, until the Lord will show you the mercy which you desire. Only do not be negligent. Fear not, for the Lord, Who has placed you in this work, will put it in order, and we will share the concern with you.

329.

Q: I beg you, my Father, tell me in what way I should correct (others), and in what cases I should act the fool, that is, pretend that I do not understand the matter and pay no attention to it?

A: Concerning others, act thus: when you know that the one who sins is sensible and accepts your words, in exhorting him, say: "Brother! If we do the work of God with negligence, this is perdition for the soul. Well, did you do well just now? Strive in future (to correct yourself)." But if he is foolish, tell him: "Believe me, brother, you are deserving of chastisement for your negligence, and as soon as I tell the Abba, he will severely chastise you." As to when you may pretend not to understand, this depends on the fault of the brother; and if it is not great, give the appearance of not understanding it; but if it is great, then you should not pretend not to understand.

330.

Q: If one of the brethren or one of the sick should sin, and I, desiring to correct him, tell him something with disturbance: should I later bow down to him (asking for forgiveness)? If it should happen that he leaves the infirmary being angry at me, what should I do? And in general, for what faults should one make a prostration (to the other)? For pride and self-justification darken the mind. And when one makes a prostration, vainglory again finds an occasion for itself.

A: Do nothing with disturbance, because evil does not give rise to good. But endure until your thought should become calm, and then speak in peace. And if the brother should listen to you—well and good; but if not, tell him: "Would you not like me to reveal this to the Abba, and we will do as he judges," and you will be at peace. But if he goes away angry, tell the Abba, and he will enlighten him: but make no bow to him (that is, do not beg forgiveness), for through this you will give him occasion to think that you are actually guilty before him, and he will arm himself against you even more. But from other people be careful to ask forgiveness, corresponding to the sin: as soon as you see that your sin is great, bow down; but when it is not great, say with your lips, with a feeling of heartfelt repentance: "Forgive me, brother." Beware of pride and self-justification, for they hinder repentance; and it also happens that a man gives a bow out of vainglory. Despite these three passions (pride, self-justification, and vainglory); where necessary, make a bow with humility, fear of God, and understanding. According to your strength, strive to remain in these virtues, and God will help you, by the prayers of the Saints.

339.

Q: Tell me, my Father, what should be the degree of mutual love of one brother to another?

A: Brother! One thing is the love of the Fathers for their children, and another the love of the brethren for their brothers. The love of spiritual Fathers for their children has nothing harmful or fleshly in it; for they are confirmed in spiritual wisdom, and both in word and deeds they strive always and in everything to give benefit to the young. Loving them in this way, they are not silent before them about their deficiencies; but they often accuse, exhort, and comfort, as a good father exhorts his children. For to them it is said: "Accuse, forbid, entreat" (II Tim. 4:2), as often your Abba acts with regard to you, even though you do not understand when he accuses, forbids, and comforts you, and when out of love he is not silent about your transgressions. By this it is revealed that his love toward you is spiritual. Everyone, according to his own measure, loves his neighbor; but the degree of perfect love is this: that for the sake of the love which a man has for God, he loves also his neighbor as himself. Youth should guard itself in everything: for the devil quickly hinders the young. At first they begin in conversation to speak as it were for spiritual profit, or not even for this; but later they pass over to something else, to irritation, to idleness, to laughter, to slander and to other evils, so that in them are fulfilled the words: "Having begun in the spirit, ye now finish in the flesh. This all ye suffer in vain" (Gal. 3:3, 4). Just in this way are the young subjected to a fall, from senseless love for each other, and because they gather together for special conversations.

Their degree of love for each other should be such: not to slander each other, not to hate each other, not to belittle, not to seek only one's own, not to love one another because of bodily beauty or any bodily occupation, not to sit with each other without extreme need, so as not to fall into over-boldness, which destroys all the fruits of a monk and makes him like dry wood. This is the degree of the love of the young for each other. And just as they themselves should beware of over-boldness and idle talking, so should they guard their brethren, fearing to sit with each other inopportunely so as not to be caught in those nets nor catch their brethren, fearing the one who said: "Woe unto him that giveth his neighbor drink with a cloudy venom" (Heb. 2:15 q.v.). And again: "Evil conversation corrupteth good manners" (I Cor. 15:33). Pay heed to yourself, brother!

341.

Q: Another brother asked the same Elder: "Abba, I desire to be saved, and I do not know the path of salvation. A thought says to me: Why do you live here in the community without doing anything? Go to another place. How should I act in this case?"

A: Brother! Through the Divine Scripture and the Fathers, God has indicated to us the path of salvation, saying: "Ask thy father and he will inform thee, thine elders, and they will tell you" (Deut. 32:7). And so, if you wish not to go astray under the pretext of humility, agreeing with the thought (that says) to go away from here to a place where you will obtain benefit—then do nothing without asking the spiritual Fathers, and you will not go astray by the grace of God, "Who wisheth all men to be saved and to come to the knowledge of the truth" (I Tim. 2:4).

342.

Q: The thought tells me that if I go away somewhere and begin to be silent, I will finally acquire perfect silence. Being a debtor in many sins, I desire to be delivered from them. How should I act, my Father?

A: Brother! A man who is in debt, if he does not first pay his debt, wherever he will go, whether to a city or village, or wherever he might settle—he is a debtor and does not have the freedom to remain peacefully anywhere. When he will be burdened by reproaches from men, he will be ashamed, and then somehow he will pay his debt; and being delivered from it, he can boldly and completely without fear walk among people and live where he desires. Likewise, one who strives according to his strength to bear patiently reproaches, dishonor, and deprivations for the sins he has committed, will become used to humility and labor, and for their sake his sins will be forgiven him, according to the word of Scripture: "See my humility and my labor, and forgive all my sins" (Ps. 24:18). Reflect also on this: that before the Cross, our Master Jesus Christ endured many insults and reproaches, and only after this ascended the Cross. Similarly, no one can attain perfect and greatly-fruitful silence and holy and perfect repose, if first he does not suffer with Christ and endure all this suffering, remembering the words of the Apostle: "If we suffer with Him, we will be glorified with Him" (Rom. 8:17). Do not be deceived: there is no path to salvation apart from this.

344.

Brother! Let us pay heed to ourselves with fear of God, and if the merciful God, in His love of mankind, will lighten our warfare, then also we will not be negligent: for many, when it became easier, were negligent over themselves and fell headlong. But we, when it becomes easier, will give thanks to God, (remembering) from what He has delivered us, and we will remain in prayer, so as not to fall again into the same passions, or into other ones. Thus, if one has eaten something and his stomach begins to hurt, or his spleen or kidneys, and then, thanks to the diligence and knowledge of the physician, he is healed—he will no longer give himself over to negligence over himself, remembering the past danger, so as not to fall into a worse condition, just as the Lord said to the one He healed: "Behold, thou art healed; in future sin no more so that it will not be worse with you" (John 5:14).

347.

Q: If before the soul there are two harmful things, and it is absolutely impossible to avoid one of them, what should one do?

A: Of two harmful things, one should choose the less harmful. In the stories of the Fathers it is written: Someone came to ask of another a dinar, and the other did not give it, saying: "I have nothing to give you." When he was asked why he did not give it to him, he replied: "If I had given him one, it would have caused harm to his soul, and therefore I preferred to violate one commandment rather than allow something ruinous for the soul."

348.

Labor to acquire thanksgiving toward God for everything, and the power of the Most High will overshadow you, and then you will find peace.

353.

Q: I was sent on business to the Holy City (Jerusalem), and from there I went down to pray at the Jordan, without asking permission for this from the Abba. Did I do well or not?

A: Without being commanded, one should not go anywhere. That which we do according to our own thoughts, even if it seems good to us, is not pleasing to God. But in keeping the commandment of your Abba who sent you is both prayer and pleasing to God, Who said: "I came down not to do My own will, but the will of the Father Who sent Me" (John 6:38).

361.

If it happens (in some case) that you do not have at hand one from whom to ask counsel, then, naming your Elder, pray thus: "God of ____ (Elder)! Do not allow me to incline away from Thy will and the counsel of Thy slave, but instruct me how to act." And what God shall inform you, that do.

362.

Q: My Master! How many times should one pray so that one's thoughts might receive assurance about this?

A: When you cannot ask the Elder, one should pray three times about every matter, and after this look to see where the heart is inclined, even though it might be fallen, and act in this way. For (this) assurance is noticeable and in every way understandable to the heart.

363.

Q: How should one pray these three times—at different times, or all at the same time? For it also happens that one cannot put off some matters.

A: If you have free time, pray three times in the course of three days; but if there is extreme need, when there is a difficulty, as at the time of the Savior's betrayal—then take as your example that He went away three times for prayer and prayed pronouncing the same words three times (Matt. 26: 44). Even though, as it seemed, He was not heard, for it was absolutely essential that that dispensation should be fulfilled, still by this example He instructs us also not to become sorrowful when we pray and are not heard at that time; for He knows better than we what is profitable for us. But in any case let us not leave off giving thanks.

364.

Q: And if after prayer I do not quickly receive assurance, what should I do? And when this happens by my own fault, but is hidden from me, how can I understand this?

A: If after the third prayer you do not receive assurance, know that you yourself are to blame for this; and if you do not recognize your transgression, reproach yourself, and God will have mercy on you.

369.

Q: A thought instigates me not to ask the Saints so as to understand what is profitable, lest, having disdained this in my infirmity, I should sin.

A: This thought is very harmful; in no way listen to it. For one who, having understood what is profitable, sins, condemns himself in every way; but he who sins without having understood what is profitable, never condemns himself, and his passions remain unhealed. And this is why the devil instils in him (such a thought), so that his passions will remain unhealed. But when the thought instils into you that you cannot fulfill the answer [of the Elder] out of infirmity, then ask in this way: "My Father! I desire to do such and such; tell me what is profitable, although I know that even if you tell me I cannot fulfill and keep what is said; but I wish to learn only so as to condemn myself for having disdained what is profitable." This will lead you to humility. May the Lord preserve your heart by the prayers of the Saints. Amen.

370.

Q: Another brother asked the same Elder [John] : "What is false knowledge?"

A: False knowledge is believing one's own thought, that the matter (in question) is exactly as it seems. Let one who desires to be delivered of this not believe his own thought in anything, but ask his Elder about everything. When the answer of the Elder turns out to be in agreement with what the brother thought, even then he should not believe his own thought, but should say: "I was mocked by the demons who instigated me to submit to the thought, as if I have true understanding, so that when I believe them they throw me down entirely into another evil. But the Elder spoke the truth, because he speaks by God's instigation, and he is in no way mocked by the demons."

372.

Q: You once said to me that both in asking about thoughts and in the deeds themselves it is good to act freely; therefore, explain to me now: In what does freedom in asking consist?

A: Freedom (in asking) about thoughts consists in this: that the questioner bare his thought completely to the one he asks and hide nothing from him, that he change nothing out of shame, and likewise not express his thought as if it came from someone else, but as from himself, as is befitting; for pretense is more harmful than anything else.

378.

Q: When I ask concerning subtle thoughts, my mind thinks highly of itself, as if I were investigating them in detail.

A: If you wish to ask certain of the Fathers concerning subtle thoughts, and not to think highly of yourself at the same time, remember that first of all there is required of a man the correction of crude thoughts, which are forbidden by the Apostle: "adultery, impurities, envy" (Rom. 13:13), and the like, and then (is required) not to despise subtle thoughts either. He who strives after subtle thoughts and is negligent of crude ones is like a man whose house is unclean and filled with diverse junk, with fine dust in its midst; and thinking to clean it, he begins to take out of the house first the fine dust, but leaves the stones and other things over which he stum-

bles. If he removes only the fine dust, thereby the house will
not yet receive a good appearance; but when he removes the
stones and other objects, he will not leave the dust, for it
also gives a bad appearance. Therefore our Savior reproached the Pharisees and Sadducees, saying to them: "Woe to
you, because ye tithe mint, and anise, and cummin, and have
left the weightier things of the law; these things ye ought to
have done, and not leave those undone" (Matt. 23:23).

391.

Q: It often happens that the fear of God comes to my mind
and, remembering the Judgment, I immediately am filled
with tender feeling. How should I accept this remembrance?

A: When this comes to your mind, that is, when you feel
tender feeling over that in which you have sinned in knowledge or in ignorance, then be attentive, lest this occur by
the action of the devil, for your greater condemnation. And
if you ask how to distinguish true mindfulness from that
which comes from the action of the devil, then listen: when
such mindfulness comes to you and you strive to show correction in deeds, this is true mindfulness, through which sins
are forgiven. But when you see that, having remembered (the
fear of God and the Judgment) you have tender feeling,
and then again fall into the same things, or into worse sins,
let it be known to you that such a remembrance is from the
adversary, and that the demons are putting this into you for
the condemnation of your soul. Behold two clear paths. And
so, if you desire to fear condemnation, flee the works which
it does.

402.

Q: Can the demons communicate anything good? And how
does one discover that it is demonic? And what distinguishes
it from something good from God?

A: To someone it might seem that he receives something
good, but this is from the evil one for his deception. For

every good thing which comes from the devil for the deception of a man, being precisely examined, turns out to be unreal; for the devil is a liar, and there is no truth in him (John 8:44), as is shown by the consequences of that (false good). His light ends in darkness, according to the Apostle's word which speaks about diabolic heralds transformed into the servants of righteousness "whose end will be according to their deeds" (II Cor. 11:15); and the Savior says: "From their fruit ye shall know them" (Matt. 7:16). If you investigate with understanding and judgment, you will find in the false good (which comes) from the devil, there was not even a trace of good, but either vainglory, or disturbance, or something similar; but the good which comes from God always increases enlightenment and humility of heart and gives a man quietness. But when, out of ignorance, we suffer in something from the deception of the evil one, and later we recognize in this a temptation, then let us call ourselves and hasten to Him Who is powerful to do away with this temptation. One should know that to some the difference [between the good of the devil and that of God] is understandable from the very beginning; while to sinners, only at the end (of the temptation), just as a skilled master in gold work can take gold (in his hand) and tell before it is tested with fire of what sort it is, while an unskilled one does not find this out until it has been tested with fire.

404.

Q: When it seems to me that some matter will be according to God, but a thought opposes me, hindering the fulfillment of the matter, saying it is not good: how can I find out whether it is really good?

A: When it seems to you that some matter will be according to God, and a contrary thought opposes it: from this itself it is revealed whether it is according to God. For if at the time when we pray, our heart is confirmed in the good, and this good increases and does not decrease, then, whether the contrary thought which saddens us will remain or not, we know that this matter is according to God; for the good is unfailingly opposed by affliction from the envy of the devil, but by prayer the good increases. But if the seeming good is instigated by the devil, and at the same time there is an opposition proceeding likewise from him, then the false good itself decreases, and together with it the false opposition; for the enemy pretends that he is opposing the thought instilled by himself only so as to deceive us thereby into accepting this thought as good.

405.

Q: How can this be? When something good is without sorrow, can it be that it is not according to God? And when it happens that one is to perform a small benefaction, and one's thought does not encounter sorrow, can it be that what I have done is premature and not pleasing to God? I beg you, my Father, enlighten my heart.

A: If, having done a good deed, one sees that his thought does not encounter sorrow, then he should not be careless, as if the deed will pass without sorrow; for every good deed belongs to the path of God, and unlying is He Who said: "Narrow and sorrowful is the path leading to life" (Matt. 7: 14). If sorrow does not happen in the midst of a good deed, then after it it is not possible for a man not to sorrow. . . . One with understanding always expects to encounter sorrow, if not today then tomorrow, and he is not disturbed. "I prepared myself," says the Scripture, "and was not disturbed" (Ps. 118:60). And blessed is he who always has before his eyes that "the earth is the Lord's and the fullness thereof" (Ps. 23:1), and keeps in mind that God is powerful to arrange for His slaves as is pleasing to Him. Such a one does not regret what he has used for good deeds. And so, if we encounter sorrow, let it be known to us that God allows it for our testing; for He never disdains those who fear Him, and especially those who do good for the sake of His name.

407.

Q: When I do something good, how should I humble my thoughts? And how does one reproach oneself after doing something good?

A: For humility of thoughts, even though you might have performed all good deeds and kept all the commandments, remember Him Who said: "When you have done all this, say that we are unprofitable slaves, for we were obliged to do what we have done" (Luke 17:10)—and all the more when we have not even attained as yet to the fulfilling of a single commandment. Thus one should always think and reproach oneself at every good deed and say to oneself: I do not know whether it is pleasing to God. It is a great work to do according to God's will, and yet greater to fulfill the will of God: this is the joining of all the commandments; for to do something according to God's will is a private matter and is less than fulfilling the will of God. Therefore the Apostle said: "Forgetting what is behind, and stretching forth to what is ahead" (Phil. 3:13). And no matter how much he stretched out to what was ahead, he did not stop and always saw himself as insufficient, and he advanced; for he said: "Whatever is perfect, think on this" (Phil. 3:15), that is, so as to advance.

409.

Q: If it happens that I show longsuffering in some matter, my thought becomes high-minded; how should I be thinking about this?

A: When you happen to do something good, you should know that this is a gift of God, given to you by God's goodness; for God has mercy on all. But pay heed to yourself, lest in your weakness you lose the mercy revealed in you by Him, which is extended to all sinners also. That which is given you by the Lord for good, do not lose in evil; and this gift is lost when you praise yourself as one who is longsuffering and forget God your Benefactor. Besides this, you draw also judgment upon yourself as soon as you presume to ascribe to yourself that for which you should send up thanksgiving to God the lover of mankind. The Apostle says: "What do you have that you have not received? And if you have received it, why do you boast as if you had not received it?" (I Cor. 4:7). To the thought that praises you for anything, say: "Those who travel on the sea, even during a time of calm do not forget that they are still on the deep, but they always expect storms, dangers, and drowning; and the short time of calm that happens to come brings them no full benefit, because they consider themselves out of danger only when they come to harbor. And it has also happened with many that their ship has drowned them at the very entrance to the harbor. So also a sinner, while he remains in this world, should be always afraid of drowning." And so never be deceived into believing the thought that praises you for a good deed. Everything good is of God, and because of our negligence we cannot guarantee ourselves that it will remain with us. And how, after this, can we presume to be high-minded?

410.

Q: If I say to the thought, desiring to humble it, that this longsuffering was not from God, but from the evil one, unto deception, so as to draw me into high-mindedness, will I not anger God by this, since God is the source of everything good?

A: It is not harmful to say that this is not from God: God is not angered by this, because this is said by you for the overthrowing of an evil thought. One of the Saints said to certain brethren who came to him that when they were on the way their donkey had fallen. Being astonished at this, they asked how he had found this out? He replied to them: "The demons told me," even though this had been revealed to him from God. He replied thus, however, for their benefit, and therefore by this he did not anger God.

413.

Q: Tell me, Master, how can the devil dare in a vision or a fantasy during sleep to show the Master Christ or Holy Communion?

A: He cannot show the Master Christ Himself, nor Holy Communion, but he lies and presents the image of some man and simple bread; but the holy Cross he cannot show, for he does not find means of depicting it in another form. Inasmuch as we know the true sign and image of the Cross, the devil does not dare to use it (for our deception); for on the Cross his power was destroyed, and by the Cross a fatal wound was given him. The Master Christ we cannot recognize by the flesh, which is why the devil tries to convince us by lying that it is He, so that having believed the deception as if it were truth, we might perish. And thus, when you see in a dream the image of the Cross, know that this dream is true and from God; but strive to receive an interpretation of its significance from the Saints, and do not believe your own idea. May the Lord enlighten the thoughts of your mind, O brother, so that you might escape every deception of the enemy.

414.

Q: A thought says to me: "If the holy Cross appears to you, you, being unworthy of this, will fall into high-mindedness." This thought brings fear and terror upon me.

A: Do not be disturbed about this, because, if the holy Cross will truly appear to you, it will abolish the pride of high-mindedness: where God is, there is no place for evil.

415.

Q: I have heard that if one and the same dream appears to someone three times, one should recognize it as true; is this so, my Father?

A: No, this is wrong; such a dream also one need not believe. He who has appeared once to anyone falsely can do this three times and more. Watch, lest you be put to shame (by the demons), but pay heed to yourself, brother.

416.

Q: Sometimes I see in my heart that evil thoughts surround my mind like wild beasts, but cannot at all harm me. What does this mean?

A: This is a deception of the enemy, in which is concealed high-mindedness, with the aim of convincing you that evil thoughts cannot harm you in the least, so that thereby your heart might become exalted. But be not deceived by this, but rather remember your infirmity and sins, and call for aid against the enemy on the holy Name of God.

422.

Q: When it seems to me that my thought is silent and is not sorrowing, is it good then also to be instructed in the invocation of the Name of the Master Christ? For the thought says to me: "Now, when we are in peace, there is no need for this."

A: We should not think that we have this peace, as long as we acknowledge ourselves as sinful, for it is said (in the Scripture). "There is no peace for sinners, saith the Lord" (Is. 48:22). And if there is no peace for sinners, what kind of peace is this? Let us have fear, for it is written: "When they shall say Peace and safety, then shall sudden destruction come upon them, as the pains upon her that is with child, and they shall not escape" (I Thes. 5:3). It happens, however, that the enemies, with cunningness, grant the heart for a short time to feel quietness, so that the invocation of the Name of God might cease; for it is not unknown to them that from the invocation of Him they are made powerless. Knowing this, let us not cease to call to our aid the Name of God: for this is prayer, and the Scripture says: "Pray without ceasing" (I Thes. 5:17). And that which is without ceasing has no end.

423.

Q: When men praise me, or a thought in the heart, and this oppresses me, how should I act with regard to this thought?

A: When a thought praises you and you cannot escape harm, strive to call on the Name of God, and say to your thought: The Scripture says, "My people, those who bless you deceive you and trouble the steps of your feet." And that such praise, my brother, is nothing else than deception, hear the Prophet, who speaks of this, saying, "Every man is as grass and all glory of a man is as the flower of the grass" (Is. 40:6). And that he who accepts human praise does not receive benefit, of this the Master Himself speaks: "How can you believe in Me who receive glory from men?" (John 5:44). And if something does happen which is according to God, we should remember what has been said: "He who is praised, let him be praised in the Lord" (II Cor. 10:17), for the Apostle, having attained a high measure, did not praise himself but cried out, saying, "By the grace of God I am what I am" (I Cor. 15:10). To Him alone may there be glory and splendor unto the ages. Amen.

424.

Q: If, during the time of psalm-singing, or prayer, or reading, a bad thought comes, should one pay attention to it and leave off (for a while) the psalm-singing, prayer, or reading in order to oppose it with pure thoughts?

A. Disdain it and enter more carefully into the psalm-singing, prayer, or reading, so as to gain strength from the words you pronounce. But if we shall begin to be occupied with hostile thoughts, we will never be in a condition to do anything good, heeding what the enemy instils. But when you see that his cunning fabrications hinder psalm-singing, prayer, or reading, even then do not enter into dispute with them, because this matter is beyond your strength; but strive to call on the Name of God, and God will help you and do away with the cunning of the enemies, for His is the power and the glory unto the ages. Amen.

447.

Q: A brother asked the Great Elder: "Be merciful, tell me how I can be saved? For I have firmly resolved in my mind to [accept] what you will write me in your epistle."

A: If you truly desire to be saved, then show obedience in very deed; separate your feet from the earth, raise your mind to heaven, and may your instruction be there day and night. As much as you can, belittle yourself day and night, force yourself to see yourself beneath every man. This is the true path, and there is none other beside it for one who desires to be saved in Christ Who strengthens him. May he who desires (salvation) run (on it), may he who desires run, may he who desires run—may he "run that he may attain"; I testify of this before the living God, Who wishes to give life eternal to everyone who desires it. If you also desire it, brother, labor.

448.

Q: Why did the Great Elder repeat three times the words: "May he run"?

A: The Elder three times repeated these words in order to show you the indispensability of this path, and that there is none other more needful.

449.

Q: I beg you to explain to me: why on Pentecost do despondency and sleepiness overcome me more than usual?

A: This happens to us because we are more like lakes than springs; that is, we are infirm and not strong in remaining in the same condition. In addition, this sometimes depends on changes of the air, and the lengthening of the days. However, the perfect Fathers are not subject to this.

452.

Q: Someone asked one of the Elders to eat food with him, but he declined, saying that he could not. But another one asked him just to perform prayer in his cell; and when the Elder came to him, he compelled him to remain to eat food with him; and the Elder, being inclined by forceful entreaty, remained. Finding out about this, the one who had asked first was greatly saddened; is this sorrow according to God?

A: When anyone is disturbed or saddened under the pretext of a good and soul-profiting matter, and is angered against his neighbor, it is evident that this is not according to God: for everything that is of God is peaceful and useful and leads a man to humility and to judging himself. The Scripture says: "A righteous man accuses himself at the beginning of his speech" (Prov. 18:17). If anyone supposes that he desires something according to God, and if when someone begins to hinder him in this he condemns the one who hinders and reproaches him, through this it is revealed that his intent was not according to God, for the Scripture says: "From their fruits ye shall know them" (Matt. 7:16). But he whose intent is according to God, when he encounters an obstacle in anything, is rather humbled, acknowledges himself as unworthy, and considers as a Prophet the one who hinders him, supposing that he hinders him as if foreseeing his unworthiness. . . . He who has humility does not seek that his desire always be fulfilled, but he constantly strives downward—to humility.

455.

Q: What is familiarity and unfitting laughter?

A: Familiarity is of two kinds: one proceeds from shamelessness and is the root of all evils; and the other proceeds from a happy mood, and this latter is not at all profitable for the one who has it. But since only the firm and strong can avoid both of these, while we, because of our infirmity cannot do this, therefore we allow sometimes that familiarity that proceeds from a happy mood, keeping watch lest through it we give a brother an occasion for scandal. Those who are among men, if they are not perfect, cannot yet be delivered from this second kind of familiarity. And if we cannot, then let this serve for us as instruction and not as a scandal, especially when we try to cut short a conversation bound up with this; because loquacity is not very profitable, even though in appearance it might not have in itself anything unbefitting.

The same thing should be said concerning laughter, for it is the offspring (of familiarity). In one to whose familiarity is joined foul language, it is evident that his laughter also will have foulness; but if the familiarity proceeds from a happy mood, it is evident that one's laughter too will be only a happy one. But just as in general it has been said of familiarity that it is not profitable to have it, so also one should not tarry in laughter and allow oneself freedom, but one should restrain one's thought so that this laughter should pass without unbefittingness. For let those who allow themselves freedom in this know that from this they will fall into sexual sin.

456.

Q: I beg you, my Father, to tell me: what should a fitting good humor be? And how should a sinner make use of it so as not to exceed his measure?

A: The perfect are also perfectly heedful to themselves, like an artist who knows his art to perfection; even though he converses with someone while he is occupied with his work, the conversation does not hinder him from doing what is demanded by the art, and when he converses with those who are with him, his mind is entirely directed to the occupation in front of him. So also one who is conversing with others should show them a joyful face and word, while having within himself a mind that sighs. Concerning this it is written: "The sighing of my heart is ever before Thee" [Ps. 37:7]. Just as an unskilled artist is in danger of ruining his work if he converses while being occupied with it, so is it with those who give themselves over to a good mood. Such a one must have a great guarding of and heedfulness to his words and outward joyfulness of face, so as not to depart completely from the path of lamentation. Such a one, before he begins a conversation, must ask his thought how the conversation should be conducted, and through this prepare himself, for it is written: "I prepared myself and was not disturbed" (Ps. 118:60). And to prepare oneself means to distinguish the persons according to the reason for which they wish to speak to us, and to prepare one's thought in accordance with the intention of the one who comes (to us), guarding it with the fear of God. If the conversation will be for greeting, let him converse with pleasantness with words befitting this. But while receiving the Fathers, let it be dissolved with joy, according to the example of Abraham, who washed the feet of the Master and the Angels and received them with words of entreaty. The circumstances themselves will show us where and how it is fitting to use joyfulness; and therefore, when we happen to persuade a visitor to eat or drink something, let us do this with joyfulness, shortening it in order to avoid disturbance of thought.

458.

Q: A brother asked the Great Elder: "Tell me, my Father, is the contrition genuine which it seems to me that I have? Should I remain here alone? And pray for me, because bodily warfare disturbs me."

A: Brother! Your present weeping and present contrition are not genuine, but they come and go; whereas genuine weeping, joined with contrition, are the slaves of man, constantly subject to him. And he who has them is not overcome by warfare; (this weeping) erases previous sins and washes defilements and ceaselessly preserves the man who has received it by the Name of God, banishes laughter and dispersion, and supports ceaseless lamentation, for it is a shield which repels all the fiery arrows of the devil (Eph. 6:16). He who has it is not at all wounded by warfare, even if he is in the midst of men and even with harlots; but (this weeping) remains inseparably with us (who are outside the world and conducting warfare), and wages warfare for us. Behold, I have shown you the signs of infirmity and of valor. Do not think that God was in no condition to ease this warfare for you. He could do this especially for the sake of the Saints who pray for you; but loving you, He wishes by means of many battles and exercises to train you, so that you might attain the measure of advancement; but you will not attain it if you do not keep everything that has been commanded you through the writings (which I have sent you)—I, your vainglorious teacher. But so as to remain in solitude—this is a matter of (having) sufficient strength, and when you will attain this I myself will send you, but (now) I say to you: struggle, my son, as I have told you, and I believe that you will prosper in Christ. Fear not: may the Lord be with you. Amen.

459.

Q: (The same brother to the other Elder [John]): I beg you, Lord Abba, pray for me that the Lord might give me a little humility. And as the Fathers say that he who does not cut off the root of a passion will again fall into it, then how can I cut off the root of fleshly passion and gluttony and love of money? And as the Great Elder told me that my present weeping is not genuine, but comes and goes, for what reason does this happen to me? And should I compel myself to weep, or should I leave this off until true contrition comes?

A: Brother! God gives us humility, and we refuse it and again say: Pray that God might grant me humility. Humility is the cutting off of one's will in everything and having cares over nothing. And to cut off the root of those passions, as you said, means to cut off your will, cause offense to yourself as much as possible, and compel the organs of the senses to keep their order, and not misuse them; through this the root not only of these, but also of other (passions) is cut off. And concerning the fact that your present weeping is not genuine, that is, it goes away from you and again comes back, (I say): This is because your mind in turn becomes weak and becomes inflamed. But when the warmth will become constant, there is great and constant contrition, and genuine weeping follows it, over which you should take care, compelling yourself so as to receive it. Brother! Strive to preserve the words and commandments of the Elder, and you will be saved.

460.

Q: A certain Christ-loving man asked the same Elder: Should one be curious about the Divine Mysteries? And is a sinner who approaches them condemned as unworthy?

A: When coming into the holy temple to receive the Body and Blood of Christ, and when receiving Them, pay heed to yourself that you unfailingly believe the truth of this (Sacrament). But as to how this happens, do not be curious, as it has been said: "Take, eat, This is My Body and Blood." The Lord gave them to us for the remission of sins (Matt. 26: 26; Mark 14:22). We have hope that he who believes thus will not be condemned, but he who does not believe is already condemned. And thus, do not forbid yourself to approach, condemning yourself as a sinner, but recognize that a sinner who approaches the Savior is vouchsafed the remission of sins.

470.

Q: How does it happen to me that when I speak with someone on some matter, I speak with disturbance, and even though I many times repent over this, still, against my own desire, I fall again into the same thing. Also, why does despondency weigh me down?

A: This happens because our heart does not remain in (spiritual) activity, which is also why we fall into despondency and into many other forms of evil.

471.

Q: The Great Elder said that as long as one feels disturbances in thoughts, even hair-thin, this is from the evil one. Explain this to me.

A: When you think to do something and you see disturbances in the mind, and after you call on the Name of God it will still remain, even if hair-thin, know from this that what you want to do is instilled in you by the evil one, and do not do it. And when after you think of doing something, disturbance attacks you and seizes the mind, then also you should not do what you are thinking of, for nothing done with disturbance is pleasing to God. But when someone opposes (the deed to be done) with a disturbance, one need not at all regard the matter as harmful, but one should look at it to see whether it be good or not. If it is not good, it should be abandoned, and if good, you should do it, disdaining the disturbance by the help of God.

493.

Q: Abba, for the Lord's sake have mercy on me. When I rest by myself, fantasies rise up against me, and I am in anguish of soul, as if someone is attacking me, so that this continues even during sleep, and I am deprived of rest. In addition, I am fearful by nature, and warfare rises up the more strongly against me, and I can hardly get to sleep at all. And if I sleep a little, as I have said, it is with disturbance and faintheartedness, so that I feel weakness in the body and cannot even move. But you, Master, knowing what is profitable for me, do it for me, my good Father! Forgive me, a sinner and much-suffering one.

A: Brother! You should glorify God that He is justifying in you the words of Scripture, which says: "Faithful is God, Who will not leave you to be tempted more than you are able to bear" (I Cor. 10:13). According to your strength, He allows you to be trained in spiritual warfare. He tests great ones (men) in great trials according to their strength, and they rejoice in this, for trials bring a man to (spiritual) advancement. Where something good is at hand, there warfare occurs. And thus, do not fear trials, but rejoice in them, because they will lead you to advancement. Disdain this temptation. God will help you and cover you.

495.

We are praying for you; and do you, according to your strength, acquire humility and submission. Do not insist on any occasion that it should be done according to your will, for from this anger is born; do not judge and do not belittle anyone, because from this the heart grows faint and the mind is blinded, and from this negligence appears and unfeelingness of heart is born. Keep ceaseless vigil, learning in the law of God, for through this the heart is warmed by heavenly fire, as is said: "And a fire shall flame forth in my instruction" (Ps. 38:4). Do not be sad, brother; your calling is from God; do not be despondent and do not weaken. God does not demand of you what is beyond your strength, but (demands) labor to the extent possible.

497.

Q: What should I do, my Father? I suffer from sexual passion.

A: As much as you can, wear yourself out, but according to your strength; and have hope not in this, but in love from God and in His protection, and do not give yourself over to despondency, for despondency serves as the beginning of every evil.

506.

Q: Pray for me, my Father, and tell me what this means: when I wish to sing (psalms or prayers), I feel slothfulness and especially when it is cold. And therefore for many nights already I have been performing psalmody and prayer sitting. I fear that this comes from slothfulness. And so vouchsafe me, my Father, enlightenment and pray that I might fulfill all that you tell me.

A: To all it is commanded to pray one for another (James 5: 16). And as for whence comes that of which you ask, know that in part a seed from the devil is mixed in here, and in part also bodily infirmity. And so, if you will perform psalmody and prayer sitting down, but with contrition, this does not hinder your service being pleasing to God; for he who performs it even standing, but dispersed, his labor will be for nothing. May the Lord help you, brother. Amen.

532.

Q: When something seems to me good, for example, to be continent or remain in silence or do someone a good deed, or something similar, should I do this of myself, or with the counsel of the Fathers?

A: If a man does not ask counsel of the Fathers concerning a matter which seems good, the consequences will be bad, and that man oversteps the commandment which says: "Son, do all with counsel" (Sirach 32:24), and again: "Ask thy father and he will inform thee, thine elders and they will tell you" (Deut. 32:7). And nowhere will you find that the Scripture commands anyone to do anything of himself. Not to ask counsel means pride, and such a man turns out to be an enemy of God; for "God opposeth the proud, but to the humble He giveth grace" (Prov. 3:34). And who (after this) will be humble, if not he alone who bends his neck down before the Elders and accepts their counsel in the fear of God.

535.

Q: If the Abba has a correct manner of thought (about faith), but foresees that on this place a heresy will arise, and there is danger that one will be compelled to violate right faith, and the Abba does not wish to move from this place, but the brother, recognizing his own infirmity, wishes to go away to another place: does he do well, or not?

A: Before the time when a heresy arises which might bring one into a difficult situation, no one should go away, lest there be fulfilled in him the word of Scripture: "The impious one flees with no one pursuing him" (Prov. 28:1). But when it (the heresy) is revealed, then one should do this, in the fear of God and with the counsel of spiritual Fathers.

540.

Q: What shall I do, my Father; battles oppress me and ever more strongly rise up against me. Tell me, what is the sign that I have hope in God, and what is the sign of the forgiveness of sins? And how should I remain in my cell according to God?

A: Brother! The time of battles is the time of doing; do not grow weak, but do. Wage battle; and when it increases, do you also become strengthened, calling out: "Lord Jesus Christ, Thou seest my infirmity and my grief, help me 'and deliver me from those that persecute me, for I have hastened unto Thee'" (Ps. 141:7; 142:9); and pray that you might receive strength to serve God in a pure heart.

The sign of hope in God consists in casting away from yourself every thought of care for the flesh and not thinking at all that you have something in this age, for otherwise you will have hope in this, and not in God. The sign of the forgiveness of sins consists in hating them and not doing them any more. But when a man reflects on them and his heart takes enjoyment in them, or he performs them in deed: this is a sign that his sins are not forgiven him, but that he is still accused of them. To remain in one's cell according to God means to judge yourself when in your heart you take enjoyment of the beauty of your cell or your bodily repose, and to say: woe to me a sinner! I have all this for my own condemnation, and I am unworthy of it, while others who are worthy endure hardship, wandering and finding no bodily repose.

Lord Jesus Christ, forgive me for this also, for the sake of Thy Name which reproaches us. May the Lord strengthen and confirm you, my son, so that you might advance and come into the measure of perfection. Amen.

544.

Q: A brother asked the Great Elder, saying: "I have some dogmatical books, and when reading them I sense that my mind is translated from passionate thoughts to the contemplation of dogmas. But sometimes a thought forbids me to read them, saying: 'you should not read them, because you are wretched and impure.'"

A: I would not want you to occupy yourself with those books, because they exalt the mind on high; but it is better to study the words of the Elders which humble the mind below. I have said this, not to belittle the dogmatical books, but I only give you counsel; for food is diverse.

546.

Q: A brother who was in contact with Abba Barsanuphius before this Elder went into silence in the community of Abba Seridos, and then separated from him, returned and belittled a certain pious brother as an ignoramus and a negligible person, and then asked the Elder to instruct him on the previous path, saying: "God has (again) brought me to your holiness."

A: The Apostle says: "The Kingdom of God is not in words" (I Cor. 4:20), and Abba Macarius said: "One who rightly believes and struggles in piety Jesus will not give over to passions and into the hands of demons." The Lord said: "There were many widows in the days of Elijah in Israel, and to none of them was Elijah sent, but only to Sarepta of Sidon," even though she was a pagan. And again He said: "There were many lepers in the days of Elisha in Israel, and not one of them was cleansed but for Naaman the Syrian" (Luke 4:25-26), who, even though he was of another people, still believed. Therefore also I supposed that, having separated from

us, you had left off self-justification and acquired humility;
but I see from your thoughts that you are just the same, or
have become even worse. If "God hath chosen the foolish
and humble and mean of this world" (I Cor. 1:27, 28), then
it is apparent that He has rejected the glorious and those who
enjoy praise from men; for not that which is pleasing to man
is pleasing to God, but that which is dishonorable among men
for the sake of God is blessed by God, as He Himself has said
of this: "Blessed are ye when men shall separate you and hate
you and speak of your name as evil for My Name's sake: rejoice and be exceedingly glad, for thus their fathers did to the
Prophets" (Luke 6:22-23). You were trained together with us
not a little time; test your own heart: what occasion or counsel did you receive from us which would separate you from
the path of God? And whence did the covering come which
was over you if not from the grief which you endured when
banished by the Elder for your own good? Tell me, brother:
on what does God look, on a man's beginning, or on how he
finishes what has been begun? You yourself know what you
have acquired during your wandering. You likewise know that
when you used to live with me I told you: If you obey me in
one thing and contradict me in something else, then you are
doing your own will also in that in which you are obedient,
and I will not give an answer for you to God. If God has
brought you, He will direct you, if you have come of your
own will, for it is written: "I have let them go according to
the will of their hearts" (Ps. 80:13). And thus, pray for me,
and leave us in peace, and I desire in the Lord to be without
care regarding you.

548.

The Abba of this coenobium, in which other holy Elders
also dwelt, ordered that a certain thing be done; but to certain of the brethren, who kept to their own will, this seemed
burdensome, and they began to grumble. Understanding this,
the same Great Elder gave them the following answer: Bre-

thren! The Lord has said: "My sheep hear my voice, and follow after Me" (John 10:27) and the rest. And therefore, he who is a true disciple remains obedient to his Abba in everything to death, and everything that his Abba does he turns into instruction for himself, without presuming to judge what is commanded him, or to say: "Why is this? What is this for?" Otherwise he would not be the disciple of the Abba, but his judge, and all this comes from nothing else than the corrupt human will. And thus, if anyone's Abba commands his disciple to do any deed, and the latter will begin to contradict, then it is evident that he desires to insist on his own way and abolish the word of his Abba. Let such a one judge who (in this case) will be Abba: the one whose word is abolished, or he whose word remains? He who wishes to do his own will is the son of the devil, and he who does the will of such a one does the will of the devil. And even if he does his own will, even then he will not have repose. And what is comprised in this? Only disobedience, which is the perdition of the soul. And thus, he who sees that he is tempting his Abba should go away from him, so as not to lose his own soul and incur condemnation for others whom he corrupts. Not knowing whether his Abba has done well or ill, he is scandalized prematurely, because of his own will, for even if it were done according to his will, no one would be more righteous than his Abba. And when he knows better than his Abba what is profitable, why does he still remain his disciple? Let him go away, and himself teach others.

549.

Answer of the same Great Elder to one of the Fathers, who had asked: "Should I punish my back-talking disciple with a severe penance?"

My beloved brother! Know that these times "are evil." It is indisputable that punishment is good and worthy of wonder and has many testimonies in its favor; for the Scripture says: "Whom the Lord loveth, He chasteneth" (Heb. 12:6), and again: "Blessed is the man whom the Lord chasteneth" (Ps. 93:12), and the rest. But this brother is embattled by hard-heartedness; be patient and labor with him: "Reprove, rebuke, exhort him," in the words of the Apostle (II Tim. 4:2); and if he accepts this chastisement, he will again be gained. Arouse him out of the heavy sleep of hard-heartedness, for when the husk of his weeds shall grow thick, one will have to weep over him; we will weep much and inconsolably. If he will labor to uproot the weeds while they are still small blades, he can be quickly delivered from such a passion. But when these weeds become strong, the uprooting of them will be bound up with labor, struggle, and afflictions. And so, tell him that he should pay careful heed to himself.

550.

Answer of the same Great Elder to a brother who was occupied in the coenobium with carpentry, and being embattled by various thoughts, thought thus: "My staying here brings me not the least benefit, and I have received no help at all here (for my soul)."

Brother! We ourselves do not wish to be delivered from difficult days and fierce sorrows. God has given two gifts to man, through which he may be saved and may be delivered from all the passions of the outward man: humility and obedience. But we do not strive towards them; we do not desire either to remain in them or to be guided by them so as to acquire help, to be delivered from evils, and to cling to the great Physician Jesus, Who can heal us from the inflammation (of passions). Why do you gather everything evil in your treasury, become disturbed and grieve? Cease to be prone to anger, irritated and envious. Know that such ones are despised and not honored. Abandon all deviation (from the path of righteousness), bend your neck under humility and obedience, and you will receive mercy. If you will fulfill with humility and obedience what you hear (from the Fathers), the Lord will give you His good help not only in this matter, in

which you are now occupied, but He will also arrange that all
your works will be successful, for He preserves the path of
those who fear Him and covers their walking. Why are you
dissatisfied? Why are you disputing? The mercy of God will
help you if you remain constantly in the patience of God.
Die, O wretched one, for every man. Say to your thought:
"Who am I?—'earth and ashes' (Gen. 18:27) and a dog"
(Matt. 15:27). Tell yourself: "I am entirely insignificant."
Why do you foretell perdition for yourself and do not fear
God? Why are you not ashamed to say: "I have received no
help here"? Know that Satan is blinding your heart, leading
you into ingratitude, by the thought that you are not receiv-
ing any benefit in a holy place.

O senseless man! If you were not preserved by the hand
of God and the holy prayers of the Saints who are here,
where would you be now, but in the outer darkness! Where
else could you receive so much help? Nowhere. But the devil,
desiring to remove you from a true bond with the Saints,
from their covering and the benefit received through them,
sows in you a seed of death for your perdition, so that you
might be given over completely into the hands of the enemies
of truth and they might tear to pieces the lamb, I mean your
soul. Do not analyze others, belittling or mocking them; for
the enemies catch you yourself by disturbing you with this;
they harm you yourself by banishing you from the realm of
quietness and peace, of good constancy, of understanding
and of every good. Abandon this, follow my words, and I
will bear your burden, and you will receive help, mercy and
the salvation of your soul.

Brother! We are saved with difficulty. Force yourself not
to say: "What is this? Why is this? (Sirach 39:26). Why do
not I have the same as those or the others?" But diligently
labor in your small handiwork with the fear of God, and you
will receive for it not a small reward. And do not despair, for
this furnishes joy for the devil, in which may God not grant
him to rejoice, but rather may he weep over your salvation

through Christ Jesus our Lord, to whom may there be glory unto the ages. Amen.

551.

The same brother asked the other Elder: "The thought says to me: If you wish to be saved, depart from the coenobium and be trained in silence, as the Fathers have said; for I receive no benefit from work as a carpenter, and it causes me much disturbance and grief."

A: Brother! It was already said to you that it is not profitable for you to leave the coenobium, and now I repeat that as soon as you leave, a fall is waiting for you. But you yourself know what you are doing. But if you truly desire to be saved, then acquire humility, obedience and submission, that is, the cutting off of your will, and you will be alive in heaven and on earth. As for silence, of it the Fathers say: "You do not know, and indeed many do not know (in what it consists)." Silence does not consist in being silent with the lips; for one may say thousands of profitable words, and this is accounted to him for silence; while another will say a single idle word, and it is accounted to him for a trampling on the teachings of the Savior; for He Himself has said: "Ye will have to give account in the day of Judgment for every idle word which cometh from your lips" (Matt. 12:36). You say that from occupying yourself with carpentry you receive no benefit; but believe me, brother, that you yourself do not know whether you receive benefit (or not). And this is nothing else than a mocking by the demons, who show your mind what they want, in order that you might do your own will and disobey your Fathers. He who wishes to be confirmed in the truth asks the Fathers whether something or other is harmful or profitable for him; he believes what they say and does what brings him benefit. Many have given payment so as to be reproached and become accustomed to patience, but you are learning patience even without money according to the word of the Lord: "In your patience possess ye your souls"

(Luke 21:19). We should give thanks to the one who offends us, because through him we acquire patience. You are in a good place that the devil might not tempt you; may the Lord help you. Amen.

556.

Q: A brother asked the same Elder: "When I hear of someone that he is speaking ill of me, what should I do?"

A: Immediately stand at prayer and pray first for him, then for yourself, saying: "Lord Jesus Christ! Have mercy on this brother and on me, Thy useless slave, and protect us from the evil one, by the prayers of Thy Saints." Amen.

578.

Pay firm heed to yourself and do not forget again to preserve unfailingly in the memory what I have told you, and do not give yourself over to negligence, for many even after they have acquired gold and have sealed it have given themselves over to negligence and have lost what was sealed. If a man does not fertilize and sow his earth for the reception of rain, then no rains which water it will help it to give fruit.

583.

Abba Elian (a new abbot) said to the Elder: "My Father! I am a beginner and know nothing. What do you command me to tell the brethren?"

A: Tell them the following: "The Lord Jesus, Who said 'I will not leave you orphans; I will come to you' (John 14: 18), will take care for you; and do you pay heed to yourselves with all humility of wisdom and love towards God, and He will bless you and will be for you a covering and leader." Tell them likewise: "No one should conceal a thought; for if one conceals thoughts, the evil spirits rejoice, striving to destroy his soul." And if any of the brethren reveals his thought to you, then call out mentally: "Lord! Grant me what is pleasing to Thee for the salvation of the soul (of the brother), so that I might tell it to him and might tell Thy word and not mine"; and then say what comes to your mind, saying to yourself: "This is not my word, for it is written: 'If one speaks, it is the words of God' (I Peter 4:11)."

587.

Q: When one of the brethren sins, how should he be accused: apart, or in front of the brethren?

A: When the fault is great, then in front of the brethren, but first you should say to him: "If you do not correct yourself, I will declare this before the brethren." Thus the Lord has commanded: "Accuse him between yourself and him alone, and if he be converted you will have gained your brother; but if not, then take another with you, or two" (Matt. 18:15), and the rest. But when the sin is small, accuse him in private, and besides this place a penance (on him).

588.

Q: In what does one save his soul who lives in the coenobium with patience? And what advantage does he have who lives in a place where there are Holy Fathers?

A: He who dies in humility and obedience is saved by Christ; for the Lord Jesus is his defender. But when one keeps to one's own will, even though sometimes he does take on himself the mask of obedience and humility, he answers for himself. Such a one, who lives according to his own will for the sake of bodily repose and not for the sake of profit for the soul, should be exhorted from time to time, for the sake of Him Who wishes "all men to be saved and come to the understanding of the truth" (I Tim. 2:4). If he will continue to keep his own will, one should endure him, until he becomes ashamed or abandons his own will. But if he causes harm to the brethren, one must declare to him: "If you continue to act thus, you cannot remain in this brotherhood"; for by the natural (order of things) itself a man cannot tolerate that there should be repose for one with harm for many. But he who remains in the monastery with good faith and according to God, receives protection from God and edification, and when one who has such an activity dies, he inherits (eternal) repose. As for the advantage which he receives who lives in a place where Holy Fathers live, it consists in having faith with good deeds, and believing in the power of the Fathers, for "the prayer of a righteous man availeth much" (James 5:16), something which one cannot find everywhere.

589.

The Elder declared the following to the brethren (concerning patience and obedience):

"Brethren, you have come here not for repose but for sorrow, for thus did the Lord command to the Apostles: 'Ye shall have sorrow and grief on the earth' (John 16:33). If you will follow the Lord Jesus, He also will remain with you; but if you renounce Him, He also will renounce you. He who desires to receive a blessing from God listens to Him, as He Himself has said: 'He that keepeth My word will not die forever' (John 8:51). And he who seeks eternal life strives to keep this word unto the shedding of blood, that is, to cut off his own will, for no one who seeks his own will is pleasing to God nor has any part with Christ. And thus, pay heed to yourself with fear of God, and the Lord will cover you with the prayers of the Saints. Amen."

590.

Q: Tell me, my Father, how I should meet visitors: laymen, Fathers and brothers.

A: Entering into wisdom, receive everyone without causing scandal to anyone, according to the example of the Apostle, who said that he was pleasing both to the Jews and to the Greeks and to the Church of God (I Cor. 10:32). For the sake of Christ's love, I shall remind my lord, that our times have degenerated to bodily repose and the filling of the belly, which give birth to all the passions; guard yourself from those who come for such an occasion, whether they be laymen, or Fathers or brothers. When they come, do not feed them too much, nor refuse them entirely either; but when there is someone who comes especially for this purpose, keep away from him. You know how the Abba acts when he is with visitors; it is more profitable for you to be called "stingy" when you are not so, than to be called a "lover of pleasure". . . . Thus, be sensible with regard to visitors; you should have understanding and wisdom so as to find out about each the reason why he has come: for God or for food. Finally, as much as possible beware of conversations on fleshly things with visitors, who have no need to hear any word, unless there be one who has need to hear the Word of God (for which God will give you understanding)—with such ones converse on the lives of the Fathers, on the Gospel, on the Apostles and Prophets, and do not allow them to speak on worldly matters: for otherwise your food and everything else will be fleshly. What I have said above has no relation to fleshly teaching; and it is not fitting for you to have conversations on worldly matters, for this is fleshly teaching. Say to such a one: "Abba! The Lord said: 'Give to Caesar what is Caesar's, and to God what is God's' (Matt. 22:21); if you have come for the sake of God, you can converse on what is pleasing to God. The world loves its own; but the world does not agree with the will of God." Otherwise we shall be chastised, by conversing not according to the will of God, for the Apostle said: "Fleshly wisdom is enmity against God, which doth not submit to the will of God, nor can it" (Rom. 8:7).

620.

Where is the cutting off of your will in everything? If in one thing you cut off your will, but not in something else, then it is clear that even in that in which you cut off your will, you had another will of your own. For he who submits, submits in everything; and such a one is not full of care for his salvation, because another answers for him—he to whom he gave himself in submission and to whom he entrusted himself. And so, if you wish to be saved and live in heaven and on earth, keep this, and I will answer for you, O brother; for if you will be negligent, then see to it yourself.

667.

Q: What do the words you have spoken mean: "See to it, lest you be drawn away by a thought of sexual sin"?

A: This happens not only with regard to sexual passion, but in other cases also. The mind is subjected to this as a consequence of distraction, and when this happens a man should cry out to himself, saying: "O Lord! Forgive me for the sake of Thy holy Name; I have been subjected to this for my negligence. Deliver me from distraction and from every net of the enemy; for Thine is the glory unto the ages. Amen." And let the following be for you the sign by which you may know that you are drawn away: if one is speaking (with others) and his mind is distracted here and there, it happens that when he speaks of one thing his thought passes over to something else; this is what it is to be drawn away. Likewise, if anyone is doing something and passes over in thought to something else; in his forgetfulness he either ruins what he is doing or does something more than necessary, and this is likewise (a case of) being drawn away. In the same way a sexual thought draws us away. It happens that one is conversing with another, and if the enemy succeeds in drawing his mind away from God-pleasing sobriety, then, as a consequence of distraction, a sexual desire appears in the mind. And this is likewise a drawing away, because it has happened not from reflection or remembrance, but a man is drawn away by it out of forgetfulness. And such a one is like a traveller who, by reason of grief that comes upon him, goes away from the straight road and finds himself on another road. But coming back to himself, a man should call out to himself, according to what has been said above, and hasten to God's mercy. The

Lord is merciful and will accept him like the prodigal son; we know with what mercifulness He accepted the latter. But when this warfare arises in the mind even without distraction, one must be sober, not take enjoyment of such thoughts, not tarry in them, but all the sooner hasten to God the Master.

670.

Q: A certain Christ-loving man asked the Great Elder: "What should I do? I am quickly attracted by the passions."

A: Do not conclude an alliance with them, and "guard your eyes so as not to see vanity" (Ps. 118:37), and your hands from greed, and God will deliver you from them. Conduct yourself in an orderly way, do not eat or drink to satiety, and these passions will grow quiet in you, and you will have repose.

696.

Q: How can I acquire a heartfelt conviction that every man is righteous, or that I am more sinful than all other men? My mind has doubts in considering every man righteous.

A: Consider yourself the most sinful and the last of all, and you will have repose.

697.

Q: When I converse with someone on the Lives of the Holy Fathers and of their replies, my heart becomes high-minded. Tell me: how am I to converse with humility of wisdom; to whom should I speak about them, and with what aim?

A: When you converse about the Lives of the Holy Fathers and about their replies, you should condemn yourself, saying: "Woe is me; how am I speaking about the virtues of the Fathers, while I myself have acquired nothing of this and have not advanced at all? And I live, instructing others for their benefit; how will there not be fulfilled in me also the words of the Apostle: 'Thou that teachest another, teachest thou not thyself?' (Rom. 2:21)." And when you will speak thus, your heart will become contrite, and your words will be humble. But you examine likewise to whom it is that you are speaking. When you know that your listener receives benefit, then converse with him; but otherwise it is not needful even to speak; for it is said: "Blessed is he who speaks into the ears of the listeners" (Prov. 25:12), lest it turn out "that you give holy things to dogs, and cast pearls before swine" (Matt. 7:6). May the Lord give you understanding, brother, so that you might not deviate from the path of humility.

701.

Q: A certain Christ-loving man, who was very continent and concerned over his soul, sent to ask the same Elder: "How is it profitable for a man to ask: to do what seems good to him, or to ask the Fathers?"

A: He who thinks to do anything good of himself, without asking the Fathers, does not follow the law and does nothing lawfully. But he who acts after questioning fulfills the Law and the Prophets; for to ask is a sign of humility, and such a one imitates Christ, Who humbled Himself, taking "the form of a servant" (Phil. 2:7,8). The man who lives without counsel is an enemy to himself, for the Scripture says, "Do all with counsel" (Sirach 32:21). And John Kolov says: "If you see a young one ascending to heaven by his own will, hold him by the foot and throw him down." It is more profitable to ask with humility than to walk according to one's own will; for the Lord Himself places in the mouth of him who is asked what to say, for the sake of the humility and uprightness of heart of the one who asks.

710.

Q: If a persecution occurs, what should I do? Remain calm, or leave?

A: Ask the Spiritual Fathers, and do as they tell you; and do not follow your own understanding, lest out of senselessness you fall into misfortune.

711.

Q: And if during a time of need there are no Fathers in whom I have complete trust, so as to ask them of this, how should I act? Should I remain so as to show that I have not betrayed my faith, or leave, fearing that they may force me to betray it?

A: Stand at prayer and pray, with your whole heart to God the Lover of Mankind, crying out: "O Master! Have mercy on me for the sake of Thy goodness; do not allow me to incline away from Thy will, and do not give me over to perdition during the time of the present trial." Do this three times as also the Saviour did in the hour of His betrayal; and if after this you feel in yourself an undoubted fervor for remaining and, with the help of God's grace, for enduring all the misfortunes ahead, even unto death itself,—then remain. But if you feel fear in your heart, then leave: and do not think that by this you are betraying the faith; God does not demand of us what is above our strength. For when, feeling fear in yourself, you remain, it may happen that, not being strong enough to bear the sorrows and tortures that will come upon you, you will become a betrayer of the truth and will subject yourself to eternal torment.

713.

Q: How should one entreat the Fathers for the forgiveness of one's sins? Should one say: "Forgive me"; or: "Entreat forgiveness for me"? And when I entreat the Lord Himself, what should I say?

A: When we entreat the Fathers who have departed to the Lord, one should say: "Forgive me." But to those who are still with us, one should say: "Pray for us that we may receive forgiveness." And when you entreat the Lord Himself, speak thus: "Have mercy on me, O Master, for the sake of Thy holy martyrs and for the sake of the Holy Fathers, and by their prayers forgive me my transgressions." For the Prophet also said: "For the sake of Abraham Thy servant" (Dan.

129

3:35), and the Lord Himself said: "I will defend this city for
My sake, and for the sake of David My servant" (4 Kings
19:34).

714.

Q: When I am with worldly people and idle talking begins,
should I remain or leave?

A: If you have no special need (to remain), then leave; but if
there is need (to remain), then turn in your mind to prayer,
not judging them, but acknowledging your own weakness.

715.

Q: If they are well-disposed toward me, do you command
that I change this conversation to another, more profitable
one?

A: When you know that they will willingly listen to the word
of God, tell them something from the lives of the Holy Fathers—and change their conversation to another, soul-saving,
one.

717.

Q: How can a man pray without ceasing?

A: When one is by oneself, one should occupy oneself with
psalm-singing and pray with lips and heart; if one is at the
marketplace and in general with others, one should not pray
with the lips, but with the mind alone. At the same time one
should guard the eyes so as to avoid the dispersal of thoughts
and the nets of the enemy.

718.

Q: When I pray or occupy myself with psalmody, and I do
not feel the power of the words I pronounce, by reason of
the insensitivity of the heart: then what profit is there for me
from this prayer?

A: Even though you do not feel the power of what you pronounce, still the demons feel it, hear and tremble. And so, do
not cease to occupy yourself with psalmody and prayer, and

little by little, by God's help, your insensitivity will be turned
to softness.

731.

Q: When I see that someone is offending a monk or hurting
him, I am disturbed against him for this; do I do well or not?

A: Nothing that occurs with disturbance can be good, but it
occurs from the activity of the devil with self-justification.
And so, if you are disturbed, do not say anything, because
you will disturb him even more, and ill-will is not annihilated
by ill-will. But if you are not disturbed, tell him with meekness: "Why do you not fear sin, unjustly offending the Abba?
Or do you not know that the image which he bears is that of
God, and God is angered at you?" Speaking in this way you
will speak according to God; and God is powerful to make
him meek, as is pleasing to Him.

737.

Q: The Lord said: "Blessed are they that weep" (Matt. 5:4);
but according to the word of the Apostle we should always
be joyful (I Thes. 5:16) and accessible for all (Rom. 12:10).
Tell me what work is accounted to a man as weeping, and
what work is accounted as being always joyful? And is it possible to remain in both of these—weeping and joyfulness—
together?

A: Weeping is sorrow according to God, to which repentance
gives birth. And the signs of repentance are: fasting, psalm-
singing, prayer, instruction in the word of God. Joy is cheer-
fulness according to God, which is revealed in an orderly way
when meeting others, both in face and word. Let the heart
preserve weeping, and the face and word a befitting cheerful-
ness.

754.

Q: If one strives to do the work of God without disdaining
it, but contrary to his desire the work is ruined, is he condemned (for this)?

A: He should reproach himself and beg forgiveness from God as if he had been careless about the work.

758.

Q: Is it not sinful to do anything on Sunday?

A: To do something for the glory of God is not sinful, for the Apostle said: "working day and night, lest we burden anyone" (I Thes. 2:9); but to do anything not according to God, with disdain (for Sunday), out of greed or from forms of low love of gain is a sin. In general, it is profitable on Sundays, on the Lord's feasts and the days of commemoration of the Holy Apostles, to put away work and come to church, for the tradition of the Holy Apostles teach this.

760.

Q: My cow is sick; would it not be sensible to call someone to charm away the disease (by words)?

A: Charming is forbidden by God, and one must not resort to it in any case whatever; for to violate God's commandment is the perdition of the soul. It is better to treat your cow in some other way; ask counsel of physicians—in this there is no sin. Or sprinkle him with holy water.

764

Q: You teach that it is good on every occasion to reproach oneself. But when someone reviles me as guilty before him and I do not know of any guilt of mine, how should I act? For if I should wish to acknowledge myself guilty, this would serve as a confirmation of his bitterness against me, as if I had really sinned against him; but if, on the contrary, I begin to justify myself before him, saying that it was not so, this will be self-justification. How should I bear this reproach? Enlighten me, Holy Father, as to how I should act (in this case).

A: First reproach yourself in your heart, and make a bow to your brother, saying: "Forgive me, for the Lord's sake." And thus, with humility (not so as to justify yourself, but so as to heal him and deliver him from suspicion), say to him: "My Father! I do not realize that I wished to offend you in any way, or that I have sinned against you in anything, and therefore (I beg you) not to think of me thus." And if even after this he is not convinced, then say to him: "I have sinned, forgive me."

766.

Q: If it will be evident that it is not I who have sinned against anyone, but he has sinned more against me, how can I reproach myself? Thus, for example, if during my journey I should meet in the way a man whom I have never known, and (when meeting him) I said nothing to him, and without cause he strikes me—how can I reproach myself in this?

A: You can do so by saying: "I am guilty for having gone on this path, because if I had not gone on it I would not have met this man and he would not have struck me." Do you see that even in this case you can ascribe guilt to yourself?

767.

Q: When I do not see in myself an evident transgression, and likewise I do not find immediately something for which I should reproach myself, what should I do?

A: Say: "That I have sinned is beyond doubt, but at the present time my transgression is hidden from me." And this is what it means to reproach oneself.

770.

Q: A certain Christ-loving man asked the same Elder: "God created man free, and He Himself says: 'Without Me ye can do nothing' (John 15:5). I ask you, how can one reconcile freedom with the fact that without God one can do nothing?"

A: God created man free so that he might incline toward the good; but inclining toward it by his free will, he is in no condition to perform the good without the help of God, for it is written: "It is not of him that willeth, nor of him that runneth, but of God that showeth mercy" (Rom. 9:16). And so, when a man bends his heart toward the good, and calls on the help of God, then God, heeding his good fervor, will grant him strength for doing [good] ; and in this fashion there is at the same time both one and the other: both the freedom of man, and the help given him from God; for the good proceeds from God, but is performed through His Saints. And thus God is glorified in all, and glorifies them.

841.

Q: A bishop asked: "My Father! Since I strive to keep the fast every day until evening, therefore I ask: Tell me, is this good? and may one do anything before prayer?"

A: Regarding fasting, I shall say: Feel your heart, whether it be robbed by vainglory; and if it has not been robbed, feel it a second time, whether this fast makes you infirm in the performance of duties, for there should not be this infirmity; and if in this (the fast) does not harm you either, your fast is a correct one.

845.

Q: A certain Christ-loving man asked the Elder: "Will it be good if I shall offer the Lord Bishop what I find profitable for him?"

A: Have your heart pure before God, and then this will not harm you. And to have one's heart pure means to say nothing about anything as it were in revenge on him, but having in mind only what is good. Do not consider this a detraction: for every work that leads to correction is no detraction; while from detraction nothing good comes. But from this good consequences should come about, and therefore it is not detraction.

846.

Reply of the Great Elder Barsanuphius to the Fathers of the coenobia:

Emmanuel is interpreted "God is with us." And so, test yourselves, whether in truth God be with us. If we have removed ourselves from evils and become strangers to their inventor, the devil, then in truth God is with us. And if the sweetness of evil deeds has become bitter to us, and we take sweet enjoyment of the desire for good deeds and of having forever a dwelling in the heavens, then in truth God is with us. If we look on all men alike, and if all days (sorrowful and successful) are equal for us, then in truth God is with us. If we love those who hate us, who insult, reproach, despise, oppress us and cause us detriment just like those who love us, praise us, furnish us gain, and give us repose—then in truth God is with us. The sign of one who has attained to this measure is this: that (such a man) always has God with him, for he is always with God. If he is not with God, and God is not with him, then of necessity he will have the adversary with him; and from this the rest is clear for those who have intelligence.

848.

(No question given).

A: Write him as follows: Your entrance into the faith of Christ has brought not a little rejoicing to us and all who fear God, but it (this rejoicing) will increase yet more when we see the maturing in you of spiritual fruits. For in truth it will be joyful for us to see the fulfillment in you of that word of the Gospel: "Let your light so shine before men that they may see your good deeds and glorify your Father Who is in the heavens" (Matt. 5:16). As is known to your nobility, newly-planted trees offer many and beautiful fruits; and do you, as newly-baptized, show to all for instruction your many and splendid spiritual fruits, unto the glory of the Holy Trinity one in Essence and unto your praise before Christ-loving kings, from whom you have been vouchsafed this great gift of enlightenment (by the light of faith). And what spiritual fruits are better than struggling in the faith of Christ and giving repose to Christendom? For even though it is confirmed by Christ, still God wishes to test also the disposition of men's hearts, that it might be completely revealed towards what they are striving. It is not possible for the Church to be destroyed; for God has promised: "Upon this rock I will build My Church, and the gates of hell shall not prevail against it" (Matt. 16:18). It was necessary that a good work be done, and blessed is he through whom it is done. Exalt such blessedness, O Christ-lovers! I wish also to make this known to your nobility, that if he to whom authority is entrusted be a pagan and an adversary of the faith and should begin to act (in this spirit), it would remain for us to do nothing but close the churches until they should be opened by Christ-loving kings.

The end of the questions and answers
of Abbas Barsanuphius and John.
Glory be to our God!

TROPARION TO STS. BARSANUPHIUS AND JOHN
Tone 1

Mystical tongues of the Holy Spirit,* rational harps of grace,* sounding forth sweet hymns of discernment* which soothe and rejoice men's souls,* you moved them to cast off the yoke of passion* and to trample on Satan's head.* Wherefore, God-like Barsanuphius and wise John,* deliver those who sing to you:* Glory to Him Who hath given you grace;* glory to Him Who hath blessed you;* glory to Him Who hath saved many through your holy words of counsel.

KONTAKION, Tone 3

All the hidden secrets of men and of God's dispensation,* were revealed in the mirrors of your pure hearts.* Resplendent were the bright beams of grace that shone forth from you,* and dispelled the shadows of sin from men's souls.* Barsanuphius and John,* lights of discernment,* entreat the Lord for us all.

St. Macarius the Great with his
desert of Scetis in Northern Egypt,
showing one of the surviving monasteries.

SPIRITUAL HOMILIES

of St. Macarius the Great

PREFACE

BORN in the year 300 and reposed in 390, St. Macarius of Egypt was one of the great Desert Fathers at the dawn of monasticism. A disciple of the founder of monasticism, St. Anthony the Great, he was famous for his spiritual wisdom as well as his many miracles. The outstanding church writer I. M. Kontzevitch has written the following concerning him:

"An extraordinary and irresistible impression was produced by St. Macarius on all who came into contact with him. Divine grace transfigured his whole being. It could be noticed in his glance, in his speech, and in that extraordinary love which poured out upon all around him. His word, even the simplest, was always uttered with authority. It created and built. Filled with divine wisdom and power, it penetrated to the very depth of the human spirit. Even those who didn't know St. Macarius recognized him instantly amidst other monks by his extraordinary appearance. . . .

"The gift of love in St. Macarius attained the highest degree. His love for his neighbor was revealed especially in his condescension to the weaknesses of others. By the testimony of the Elders of Scetis, he was as it were an 'earthly god': just as God, they said, while seeing the whole world does not chastise sinners, so also Macarius covered up men's weaknesses, which as it were he saw without seeing, and heard without hearing.

" 'Christians,' he said, 'should judge no one, neither an open harlot, nor sinners, nor dissolute people, but should look upon all with simplicity of soul and a pure eye. Purity of heart, indeed, consists in seeing sinful and weak men and having compassion for them and being merciful.'

"With meekness and mildness Macarius directed his brethren, inspiring in them above all love for each other. He said: 'If, in giving someone a reprimand, you come in irritation, then you are gratifying your passion. In this fashion, without saving others you cause harm to yourself as well.'

". . . Let us cite several instructions of St. Macarius:

" 'If for you disgrace is like praise, poverty like wealth, insufficiency like abundance, then you will not die.'

" 'If we shall remember the evil that men have done us, the remembrance of God will grow weak in us; but if we shall remember the evil brought upon us by demons, we shall be safe from their arrows.'

"Asked how to pray, he replied: 'It is enough if you will often repeat from your whole heart: Lord, as it pleases Thee and as Thou knowest, have mercy on me. And if temptation comes upon you: Lord, help me! The Lord knows what is profitable for us and has mercy on us.' "

St. Macarius' *Fifty Spiritual Homilies* are a basic textbook of the principles of Orthodox spiritual life. These homilies, writes Kontzevitch, "are founded on personal experience, and therefore their language is clear, expressive, and possessed of an extraordinary imagery and power. St. Macarius' teaching is the writings of a dweller of heaven, a heavenly man. To him, who had attained perfection, the spiritual world and its laws were open. He beholds the soul and sees all that takes place in it. He indicates to it the path to perfection. He is entirely caught up in contemplation of God and in exaltation. To him the great secrets of the world above are open."[1]

Fr. Seraphim Rose began translating selected passages of St. Macarius' *Homilies* on May 9/22, 1975. They are found after *Guidance Toward Spiritual Life* in the pages of his "spiritual journal." A complete English translation of the *Homilies* by A. J. Mason had been published previously, but Fr. Seraphim had not been fully satisfied with it. In doing his own translation, he referred to the Russian version edited by St. Theophan the Recluse and published in Moscow in 1855.

Although not intended to supersede the complete English edition of the *Homilies*—which Fr. Seraphim himself was instrumental in having reprinted[2]—the present translation is valuable in that it has come down to us through the pens of two men steeped in the wisdom of the Holy Fathers and sharing their manner of life: St. Theophan and Fr. Seraphim. Also, Fr. Seraphim's choice of passages is of interest in that he was so acutely aware of the needs, problems and potentials of contemporary Christians.

We present these teachings of St. Macarius as a companion to the teachings of his successors in the desert, Saints Barsanuphius and John. As the 19th-century Holy Father St. Ignatius Brianchaninov wrote of his own awakening to the riches of Patristic wisdom: "What was it that above all struck me in the works of the Fathers of the Orthodox Church? It was their harmony, their wondrous, magnificent harmony. Eighteen centuries, through their lips, testified to a single unanimous teaching, a Divine teaching!"[3]

---

1. "The Life of St. Macarius the Great," in *The Orthodox Word*, 1969, no. 24, pp. 25-27.

2. Reprinted by Eastern Orthodox Books, P. O. Box 302, Willits, California 95490. To this edition was appended Fr. Seraphim's translation of "The Life of St. Macarius" and "The Teachings of St. Macarius" by I. M. Kontzevitch, as well as Fr. Seraphim's definitive article on the modern academic debate concerning the authorship of the *Homilies*.

3. *The Orthodox Word*, 1974, no. 58, p. 193.

ST. MACARIUS THE GREAT OF EGYPT
Commemorated January 19

Icon by Photios Kontoglou.

THE SPIRITUAL HOMILIES

Homily II

1. The evil one clothed the whole soul, this indispensable part of man, this indispensable member of him, in his malice, that is, in sin; and in this way the body became subject to suffering and corruption.

3. It is impossible to separate the soul from sin, unless God should stop and repress this evil wind which dwells in the soul and in the body. A man watches a bird flying and wishes to fly himself, but he cannot, because he has no wings. Even so, a man desires to be pure, and blameless, and without spot, and to have no vice in him, but to be always with God; but he has not the power for this. He desires to fly in the Divine air, in the freedom of the Holy Spirit; but he cannot, until he receives wings. Let us then beseech God to bestow upon us "the wings of a dove" of the Holy Spirit, that we may fly to Him and be at rest (Ps. 54:7), and that He would separate and make to cease from our souls and bodies that evil wind, sin itself, which dwells in the members of our souls and bodies.

Homily III

3. Let the object of our searching be one thing: to have in the soul a treasure, and life—that is, the Lord, in the mind.

Whether one is working, or praying, or reading, let him have that possession that passes not away, that is, the Holy Spirit.

Homily IV

8. One thing foreign to our nature, harmful passions, we have received into ourselves through the first man's disobedience, and it has taken its place as almost a part of our nature by long custom and propensity; and this foreign thing must be expelled again by that other thing foreign to our nature, the heavenly gift of the Spirit, that the original purity may be restored.

9. Every creature, whether it be angel, or soul, or demon, in its own nature is a body. Subtle though they are, still in substance, character, and image according to the subtlety of their respective natures they are subtle bodies, even as this body of ours is in substance a gross body.

17. Great and unutterable are the promises made to Christians, so great that all the glory and beauty of heaven and earth, and their adornment and variety, and wealth and comeliness and delight of things visible, bear no comparison to the faith and wealth of a single soul.

Homily V

1. Christians have their own world, their own way of life, and mentality, and word, and activity; quite different is the way of life, and mentality, and word, and activity of the men of this world. One thing is Christians, and another the lovers of the world; between the one and the other is a great separation.

Ever since Adam fell by transgressing the commandment and came under the power of the prince of wickedness, the latter does nothing but sift with thoughts of deceit and agitation all the sons of this age, and dash them on the sieve of the earth.

3. For as from one Adam all the race of men was spread over the earth, so a single taint of passion penetrated into the whole sinful race of men.

4. This constitutes the difference between true Christians and the rest of mankind, and the distance between the two is great, as we said before. The Christian mind and way of thinking is always in the heavenly frame; they behold as in a mirror the good things of eternity by reason of their partaking and having the Holy Spirit, by being born of God from above, and being privileged to be children of God in truth and efficacy, and by having arrived, through many conflicts and labors spread over a long time, at constancy, firmness, freedom from disturbance, and repose, no longer sifted and wave-tossed by unquiet and vain thoughts. By this they are greater and better than the world because their mind and the frame of their soul is in the peace of Christ and the love of the Spirit. It was of such that the Lord spoke when He said that they had "passed from death unto life" (John 5:24). Not in a form or in outward figures lies the distinguishing mark of Christians. Most men think that the difference which distinguishes themselves from the world consists in a form and in figures; and lo! in mentality and understanding they are like the world, undergoing the same shaking, and inconstancy of thoughts, and unbelief, and confusion, and disturbance, and fear as all other men. In outward form and appearance they differ from the world, and in a few points of religious ordinance; but in heart and mind they are bound with earthly bonds, never having acquired rest from God and the peace of the heavenly Spirit in their heart, because they never sought it from God, nor believed that He would vouchsafe these things to them.

5. It is in the renewing of the mind, and the peace of the thoughts, and the love and heavenly attachment for the Lord, that the new creation—the Christian—is distinguished from all the men of the world. This was the purpose of the Lord's coming: to vouchsafe these spiritual blessings to those who

truly believe in Him. Christians have a glory and a beauty and a heavenly wealth which is beyond words, and it is won with pains, and sweat, and trials, and many conflicts, and all by the grace of God. . . . Spiritual men think nothing of all this [the glory of an earthly king], because they have had experience of another glory, which is heavenly and out of the body, and have been smitten with another beauty unspeakable, and have an interest in another wealth, and live according to the inward man, and are partakers of another Spirit.

7. Very few are those who have joined a good end to a good beginning, have come through to the end without stumbling, have a single love for God alone, and have detached themselves from everything. Many come into tender feeling, many become partakers of heavenly grace, are wounded with heavenly love; but, not holding out against the diverse battles, struggles, labors and temptations from the enemy that are encountered on the way, inasmuch as each one has the desire to love something in this world and not entirely to be separated from his love, they return to various and diverse worldly desires, out of weakness and inactivity or by the cowardice of their own will, or out of love for something earthly, and remain in the world and are plunged into its miry depths. But those who truly intend to pass through the good life to the end, having this heavenly love, should not willingly receive in themselves or mix in any other love or attachment, lest thereby they hinder the spiritual, return back, and finally be deprived of life. . . . Very many men, even though they intend to receive the Kingdom and desire to inherit eternal life, still do not renounce living by their own desires and following these desires, or rather, following the vanity which has been sown in them; and without renouncing themselves they wish to inherit eternal life—which is impossible.

13. There are always needful great faith, greatness of soul, battling, patience, labors, hunger and thirst for everything good, quickness, importunity, discretion, good sense.

Very many men wish to be vouchsafed the Kingdom without labors, without struggles, without sweat; but this is impossible.

17. What now the soul has gathered within its inward storehouse shall then be revealed and displayed outwardly in the body. As trees that have got over the winter, when warmed by the unseen influence of sun and winds, put forth from within and shoot out their clothing of leaves, and as at that season flowers of the grass come forth from within the bosom of the earth, and the earth is covered and dressed, and the grass is like those lilies of which the Lord said that "not even Solomon in all his glory was arrayed like one of them" (Matt. 6:29), for these are all parables and types and figures of Christians at the resurrection.

18. To all God-loving souls, that is, to true Christians, there comes a first month, a Xanthicus, which is also called April. It is the day of resurrection; and by the power of the Sun of Righteousness the glory of the Holy Spirit comes out from within, decking and covering the bodies of the Saints— the glory which they had before, but hidden within in their souls. For what a soul has now within itself, the same then comes forth externally in the body.

20. The glory which the Saints now have in their souls, the same, as we said before, shall cover and clothe their naked bodies, and catch them into heaven; and thenceforward we shall rest, in body and soul, in the Kingdom with the Lord forever. When God created Adam, He did not provide him with bodily wings like the birds, but He had designed for him the wings of the Holy Spirit, those wings which He purposes to give him at the resurrection, to lift him up and catch him away withersoever the Spirit pleases—which holy souls even now are privileged to have, and fly up in mind to the heavenly frame of thoughts. For Christians have a different world of their own, another table, other raiment, another sort of enjoyment, other fellowship, another frame

of mind; for which reason they are superior to all other men.

21. Every one of us therefore ought to strive, and take pains, and be diligent in all virtues, and to believe, and to seek from the Lord that the inward man may be made partaker of that glory here and now, and that the soul may have fellowship in that sanctity of the Spirit, in order that we may be cleansed from the defilements of wickedness and may have at the resurrection wherewithal to clothe our bodies as they rise naked, and to robe their uncomeliness, and quicken them, and refresh them forever in the Kingdom of Heaven.

Homily VII

3. Q: Inasmuch as sin transforms itself into an Angel of light and becomes almost like grace, how can a man detect the wiles of the devil, and how can he distinguish and accept that which is of grace?

A: The things of grace are attended by joy, peace, love, and truth. Truth itself compels a man to seek truth. But every kind of sin is filled with disturbance; in sin there is no love or joy before God. Thus, endive (chicory) looks like lettuce; but one is bitter, and the other is sweet. Even in the realm of grace itself, there is what looks like truth, and there is the substance of truth itself. The ray of the sun is one thing, and the orb itself is another, and the ray does not shine in the same sense in which the light stored up in the orb does. A lamp is lighted in the house: the ray of it which beams all round is one thing, and the light in the lamp itself is another, brighter and clearer. In like manner, there are things of grace which a man sees in the distance, as if some kind of vision, and he rejoices at these visions; but it is something else when the power of God enters into him, and occupies his heart and his members, and makes his mind captive to the love of God. When they seized Peter and cast him into prison, an Angel of the Lord came, when he was shut in, and broke his chains, and brought him out; and he, like one in a trance, "thought he saw a vision" (Acts 12:9).

7. Q: Has the soul any form?

A: It has an image or form in the same way as an angel has. As the angels have an image or form, and as the outward man has an image like an angel's, and a form like that of the outward man.

Homily VIII

2. Q: Does a man enter always into this state [of grace]?

A: It is true that grace is constantly present, is rooted in and acts as a leaven in man from a young age, and this [state], being present in a man, becomes something as it were natural and inseparable, as if one essence with him. But, as is pleasing to it [grace], it changes the form of its action in man for his profit. Sometimes this fire flames out and kindles more vehemently, at other times more gently and mildly. The light that it gives kindles up at times and shines with unusual brightness; at others it abates and burns low. The lamp is always burning and shining, [but when it is specially trimmed] it kindles up from the intoxication of God's love; and then again by God's dispensation it gives in, and though the light is always there, it is comparatively weak.

Homily X

1. Souls that love truth and God, that long with much hope and faith to put on Christ completely, do not need so much to be put in remembrance by others. . . . They perceive in themselves day by day a sense of spiritual advance towards the spiritual Bridegroom. . . . Even if they are privileged through their faith to receive the knowledge of Divine mysteries, or are made partakers of the gladness of heavenly grace, they put no trust in themselves, thinking themselves to be somewhat, but the more they are permitted to receive spiritual gifts, the more insatiable they are of the heavenly longing, and the more they seek on with diligence. The more

they perceive in themselves a spiritual advance, the more hungry and thirsty they are for the participation and increase of grace; and the richer they spiritually are, the more do they esteem themselves to be poor, being insatiable in the spiritual longing for the heavenly Bridegroom, as the Scripture says: "They that eat Me shall yet be hungry, and they that drink Me shall yet be thirsty" (Sirach 24:29).

2. Such souls, which have the love of the Lord ardently and insatiably, are meet for eternal life; for which reason deliverance from the passions is vouchsafed to them, and they obtain perfectly the shining forth and participation of the unspeakable and mystic fellowship of the Holy Spirit, in the fulness of grace. But as many souls as are feeble and slack, not seeking to receive here on earth, while they are still in the flesh, through patience and longsuffering, sanctification of heart, not in part but perfectly, and have never hoped to partake in the Comforter Spirit in perfection with all conscious feeling and undoubtedness, and have never expected to be delivered through the Spirit from the passions of evil; or having at one time received the grace of God, have been deceived by sin and have given themselves over to some form of carelessness and remissness; [3.] these, as having received the grace of the Spirit, and possessing some comfort of grace in rest and aspiration and spiritual sweetness, become presumptuous at this, and are lifted up, and grow careless, without contrition of heart, and without humility of mind, neither reaching the perfect measure of freedom from passion, nor waiting to be perfectly filled with grace in all diligence and faith, but they were satisfied, and took their repose, and stopped with their scanty comfort of grace, the result of which advance to such souls was pride rather than humility, and they are at length stripped of whatever grace was vouchsafed to them, because of their careless contempt, and because of the vain arrogance of their self-conceit.

Homily XI

1. That heavenly fire of the Godhead, which Christians receive in their hearts now in this present world, that same fire which now ministers inwardly in the heart becomes outward when the body is dissolved, and recomposes the members, and causes a resurrection of the members that had been dissolved. As the fire that ministered on the altar at Jerusalem lay buried in a pit during the time of the captivity, and the selfsame fire, when peace came and the captives returned home, was renewed, as it were, and ministered in its accustomed manner, so now the heavenly fire works upon this body that is so near us, which after its dissolution turns to mire, and renews it, and raises up the bodies that had decayed. The inward fire that now dwells in the heart becomes then external, and causes a resurrection of the body.

Homily XII

1. Adam, on transgressing the commandment, suffered a twofold disaster. He lost the pure and splendid possession of his nature, which was after the image and likeness of God; and he lost also that very image in which was laid up for him according to promise all the heavenly inheritance.

2. We do not say that man was entirely lost, destroyed, and died; he died for God, but he lives by his own nature.

3. Q: How can one be poor in spirit, especially when he is inwardly conscious that he is a changed man, and has made progress, and has come to a knowledge and understanding which he did not possess before?

A: Until a man acquires these things and makes progress, he is not poor in spirit, but thinks highly of himself; but when he comes to this understanding and point of progress, grace itself teaches him to be poor in spirit, which means that a man being righteous and chosen of God does not esteem himself to be anything, but holds his soul in abasement and disregard, as if he knew nothing and had nothing, even though he knows and has. And such a thought becomes as it were a part of nature and rooted in a man's mind. Do you not see how our forefather Abraham, elect as he was, described himself as "dust and ashes" (Gen. 18:27); and David, anointed to be king, had God with him, and yet what does he say? "I am a worm and no man, a very scorn of men, and the outcast of the people" (Ps. 21:7).

4. Those therefore who desire to be fellow-heirs with these, and fellow-citizens of the heavenly city, and to be glorified with them, ought to have this humility of wisdom, and not to think themselves to be anything, but to keep the heart contrite.

5. If thou lovest the glories of men, and desirest to be worshipped, and seekest repose, thou goest off the path. You must be crucified with the Crucified One, suffer with Him that suffered, that so you may be glorified with Him that is glorified. The bride must needs suffer with the Bridegroom, and so become partner and fellow-heir with Christ. It is not permitted without sufferings, and without the rough, straight, narrow path, to enter into the city of the Saints, and be at rest, and reign with the King to ages without end.

10. Now we know that the whole creation of God is governed by God. He it was that made heaven and earth, animals, creeping things, beasts. We see them all, but do not know the number of them. What man is there that knows? God only, Who is in all things, even in the unborn offspring of the animals. Does He not know the things that are under the earth, and that are above the heavens?

11. Let us then leave these things, and rather seek, like good men of business, to gain possession of a heavenly inheritance and the things that are profitable to our souls. Let us learn to gain possessions that will stay by us. If you, who are but human, begin to search the thoughts of God and to say, "I have found out something and comprehend it," the

human mind will be found surpassing the thoughts of God. But in this you are much mistaken; and the more you desire to search and get to the bottom, the more you get out of your depth, and fail to comprehend anything. These visitations of His which happen to you—what He works day by day in you, and how—these are beyond expression or comprehension; you can do nothing but receive them with thankfulness, and believe. Have you been able to take cognisance of your own soul from the time when you were born till now? If so, declare to me the thoughts that spring up in you from dawn to dusk. Tell me the cogitations of three days. Nay, you cannot. If then you could not comprehend the thoughts of your own soul, how can you find out the thoughts and mind of God?

12. Nay, eat as much bread as you find, and leave the wide earth to pursue its way; go to the brink of the river, and drink as much as you need, and pass on, and seek not to know whence it comes, or how it flows. Do your best to have your foot cured, or the disease of your eye, that you may see the light of the sun, but do not enquire how much light the sun has, or in what sign it rises. Take that which is given for your use. Why do you go off to the hills and try to discover how many wild asses and other beasts dwell there? The babe, when it comes to its mother's breast, takes the milk and thrives; it does not search for the root and well-spring from which it flows so. It sucks the milk, and empties the whole measure; and another hour passes—the breast fills up. The babe knows nothing of it, nor the mother either, although the supply proceeds from all her members. If then, you seek the Lord in the depth, there you find Him. If you seek in the water, you find Him there, doing wonders. If you seek Him in the den, there you find Him between two lions, guarding the righteous Daniel. If you seek Him in fire, there you find Him, succouring His servants. If you seek Him in the mountain, there you find Him with Elias and Moses. He is everywhere—beneath the earth, and above the heavens, and within

us as well. He is everywhere. So too your own soul is near you, and within you, and without you; for wherever you please, in countries far away, there your mind is, whether westward or eastward, or in the skies; there it is found.

13. Let us then seek above all things to have the brand and seal of the Lord upon us; because in the day of judgment, when God will make the separation, and all the tribes of the earth, even all Adam, are gathered together, when the good Shepherd calls His own flock, all those who have the brand recognize their own Shepherd, and the Shepherd takes knowledge of those who have His own seal, and gathers them together from all the nations. Those that are His hear His voice, and go behind Him. The world is divided into two parts, and one flock is dark, which goes into eternal fire, and one is full of light, which is led up to the heavenly rest. What we now have acquired within our souls, the same then shines and is manifested and clothes our bodies with glory.

Homily XV

4. So likewise the Spirit utters warning to the soul which through grace knows God, which after being cleansed from its former sins and adorned with the ornaments of the Holy Spirit, and after partaking of the divine and heavenly food, does not behave dutifully with much discretion, and does not properly preserve benevolence and love for Christ the heavenly Bridegroom, and so is rejected and put away from the life of which at one time it was a partaker. For Satan can raise and exalt himself even against those who have reached such measures of grace as these; even against those who have known God in grace and power, malice still lifts itself up and strives to overthrow them. We must therefore strive, and watch over ourselves intelligently, to "work out our own salvation with fear and trembling," as it is written (Phil. 2:12). As many as are made partakers of the Spirit of Christ, see that you do not behave contemptuously in anything, small or great, and do not offend the grace of the Spirit,

that you may not be excluded from the life of which you have already been made partakers.

10. Q: In the resurrection do all the members rise again?

A: To God all things are easy; and He has so promised, though to human frailty and thought it appears impossible. For us God took of the dust and the earth, and constituted the body as a different kind of thing, not at all resembling the earth, and made many sorts of elements in it, such as hair, and skin, and bones, and sinews; or as a needle thrown into the fire changes its color and is converted into fire, although the nature of iron is not taken away, but still subsists; so in the resurrection all the members are raised up, and not a hair perishes, as it is written, and all become light-like, all are plunged in light and fire, and changed, and yet are not, as some say, resolved and turned into fire, with nothing of their natural substance left. Peter is Peter, and Paul is Paul, and Philip is Philip. Each one remains in his own nature and personality, though filled with the Spirit.

20 (R 18).* When the rich men of the earth have brought much fruit into their garners, they set to work again every day to get more, in order to have plenty, and not run short. If they presume upon the wealth laid up in the garners, and take things easily and add no more, but use up what they have stored already, they soon sink into want and poverty. So they have to labor and add, enlarging their intake, that they may not get behindhand. In Christianity, to taste of the grace of God is like that.

22 (R 20). If a man loves God, then God also mingles His love with him. To a man who has once had faith in God, He adds a heavenly faith, and the man becomes a twofold being. Whatever part of yourself you offer to Him, He mingles with your soul a like part of His own, that all that you do may be

---

* (R) indicates the Chapter number in the Russian edition in places where this is different from the English edition.

purely done, and your love pure and your prayer pure. Great is the dignity of man. See how mighty are the heavens and the earth, the sun and the moon; but the Lord was not pleased to rest in them, but in man only. Man, therefore, is of more value than all created things—I may venture to say, not only than visible creatures, but invisible likewise, even than the "ministering spirits" (Heb. 1:14). . . . But the material creatures are bound by an unchangeable kind of nature. 23 (R 21). Heaven was once established for good and all—the sun, the moon, the earth—and the Lord had no pleasure in them; they cannot alter from what they were created, neither have they any will. . . . But you are your own master, and if you choose to perish, you are of alterable nature. If you choose to blaspheme, to concoct poisons, to murder somebody, no one opposes or hinders you. If a man chooses, he is subject to God, and walks in the way of righteousness, and restrains his desires. This mind of ours is evenly balanced, having power to subdue by resolute thoughts the impulses and shameful desires of evil.

24 (R 22). The nature of irrational animals is bound. For example, the serpent's nature is bitter and venomous; therefore, all serpents are such. The wolf's is habitually ravenous; all wolves are of the same nature. The lamb's gentleness makes it a prey; all lambs are of the same nature. The dove is guileless and harmless; all doves are of the same nature. But man is not like that. One man is like a ravening wolf; another, like the lamb, is a prey. And both come from one and the same human race.

25 (R 23). You see how alterable this nature is. You find it inclining to evil, you find it inclining again to good. In both cases it is in a position to assent to such action as it likes. Nature, then, is susceptible both to good and evil, either of Divine grace or of the contrary power.

29 (R 27). Those in afflictions and temptations, if they endure, do not fail of the Kingdom of Heaven; therefore,

Christians in circumstances of distress are not vexed or grieved. If they are tried by poverty or suffering, they ought not to be surprised, but rather to take pleasure in poverty and reckon it as wealth, and fasting as feasting, and dishonor and obscurity as glory. On the other hand, if they should fall into circumstances which in this life are glorious, which incline them to worldly ease, or wealth, or glory, or luxury, they ought not to take pleasure in these things, but to shun them as they would shun fire.

37 (R 35). If you see a man proud and puffed up because he has a share of grace, this man, even if he should work miracles and raise the dead, but does not hold his soul worthless and contemptible, and continue poor in spirit and an object of abhorrence to himself, is cheated by sin without knowing it. Even if he works signs you cannot believe him, for the sign of Christianity is this, to be approved of God while earnestly shunning the notice of men, and even if a man has the entire treasures of the King, to conceal them, and to say continually, "It is not mine; another has put this treasure in my charge. I am a poor man, and when He pleases, He takes it from me." If anyone says, "I am rich; I have enough. I have gained; I need nothing more," he is no Christian; he is a vessel of deception and of the devil. The enjoyment of God is insatiable. The more anyone tastes and eats of Him, the more he hungers. Such men's ardor and passion for God is beyond restraint, and the more they endeavor to get on and make progress, the more they esteem themselves poor, as those that are in need and have nothing. This is what they say: "I am not fit for this sun to shine upon me." This is the sign of Christianity, this humility. 38 (R 36). But if a man says, "I am satisfied and filled," he is deceived and a liar.

39 (R 37). Q: What advantage have Christians over the first Adam? For he was immortal and incorruptible, both in body and in soul, whereas Christians die and come to corruption.

A: The real death is within, in the heart, and is concealed, and it is the inner man that perishes by it. So if anyone has "passed from death to life" (John 5:24), in that
hidden region, he does indeed live forever, and never dies.
Although the bodies of such men are dissolved for a season,
they are raised again in glory, for they are hallowed. So we
call the death of Christians sleep and repose. If the man were
immortal, and his body exempt from corruption, the whole
world, beholding the strange fact that Christian men's bodies
were incorruptible, would come over to the good by a kind
of compulsion, not by a voluntary decision.

41 (R 39). Q: Is it by degrees that evil is diminished and
rooted out, and a man advances in grace? Or is evil rooted
out at once as soon as advancement has begun?

A: As the unborn babe in his mother's womb is not at
once fashioned into a man, but the image is formed by degrees and born, and even then is not full grown, but takes
many years to develop and become a man; and again, as the
seeds of barley or of wheat do not root the moment they are
put into the ground, but cold and wind pass over them, and
then in due time the ears form; and the man who plants a
pear tree does not at once partake of the fruit; so likewise
in spiritual things, where there is so much wisdom and deli-
cacy employed, it is only little by little that a man grows
and comes to "a perfect man, to the measure of the stature"
(Eph. 4:13), not, as some say, "off with one coat, and on
with another."

49 (R 47). Conceive, then, that it is thus with the spirits of
wickedness. The world that you see around you, from the
king to the beggar, are all in confusion and disorder and
battle, and none of them knows the reason, or that it is the
manifestation of the evil which crept in through Adam's disobedience, "the sting of death" (I Cor. 15:56). For the sin
which crept in, being a kind of invisible power of Satan, and
a reality, implanted all evils. Without being detected it works
upon the inner man and upon the mind, and contends with

him by means of thoughts; but men are not aware that they are doing these things at the instigation of an alien force. They think it all to be natural, and that they do these things of their own determination, while those who have the peace of Christ in their minds, and His enlightenment, know very well the source of these movements.

Homily XVI

7. Like a bee secretly forming her comb in the hive, grace secretly forms in hearts the love of herself, and changes them from bitterness to sweetness, from hardness to softness of heart.

8. Christians are of another world, sons of the heavenly Adam, a new race, children of the Holy Spirit, shining brethren of Christ, like their Father, the heavenly shining Adam. Of that city, of that kindred, of that power, they are not of this world, but of another world. He Himself says, "Ye are not of this world, even as I am not of this world" (John 17:16).

10. There is a difference between those who have a theory and talk, but are not seasoned with the salt of heaven, who discourse of a royal table, but have never eaten or enjoyed it—and a man who has had sight of the king himself, to whom the treasures have been opened, and he has entered in, and inherited them, and eaten and drunk of the costly viands.

11. If a mother has an only son, very handsome, wise, adorned with all things good, upon whom she sets all her hopes, and it falls out that she buries him, then endless distress comes upon her, and mourning that cannot be comforted. So ought the mind, when the soul has died to God, to take up mourning and tears, endless distress, to have a contrite heart, to be in fear and care, and at the same time to have a hunger and thirst for what is good continually. Such a one passes into the hands of God's grace and of hope, and he no longer remains in that mourning, but rejoices as one

that finds a treasure, and again trembles for fear he should lose it, for the thieves are coming. Like a man who has suffered many losses by thieves, and has got away from them with much difficulty, and after this has come into great affluence and a large fortune, and has no more dread of loss because of his abundant wealth; so spiritual men, after first passing through many temptations and dreadful places, and then filled with grace and replete with good things, are no longer in terror of those who would plunder them, since their wealth is not small; yet they fear, not with the beginner's fear of evil spirits, but with fear and care how to employ the spiritual gifts entrusted to them.

Homily XVII

3. Therefore Christians are not surprised that they are to reign in that age, having already learned the secrets of grace. When man first transgressed the commandment, the devil covered the soul all over with a covering of darkness. Then grace comes and wholly removes the veil so that the soul, now cleared and regaining its proper nature, created without blemish and clear, continually beholds clearly with its clear eyes the glory of the true light and the true "sun of righteousness" (Mal. 4:2) beaming in the heart itself.

5. We must not think of these things under a single aspect and one-sidedly. So great is the repose of some men in God's grace that they become stronger than the evil that is with them, and having a gift of prayer and much repose in God, at another moment they are under the influence of evil thoughts, and are robbed by sin, though they are still in the grace of God. Light-minded and uninformed people, when grace to some extent works upon them, imagine that there is no more such a thing as sin. But those who have discretion and are prudent dare not deny that even when we have the grace of God we are liable to the influence of foul and polluting thoughts.

9. If a man clothed in beggarly garments should see himself in a vision rich, and on waking from sleep should see himself again poor and naked, so those who utter a spiritual discourse seem to speak logically enough, but if they have not the thing they discourse about verified in their mind by tasting and power and personal experience, they stand in a vain show.

Homily XVIII

5. When those who are rich in the Holy Spirit, really having the heavenly wealth and the fellowship of the Spirit in themselves, speak to any the word of truth, when they impart spiritual discourses to any and desire to gladden souls, it is out of their own wealth and out of their own treasure, which they possess within themselves that they speak, and out of this that they entertain the souls of the hearers of the spiritual discourse; and they have no fear lest they should run short, because they possess within themselves a heavenly treasure of goodness, upon which they draw to gladden those whom they are spiritually feasting. But one who is poor, and does not possess of the wealth of Christ, and has no spiritual wealth in his soul, yielding a stream of all goodness, both of words and of deeds, and of divine ideas, and of mysteries unspeakable, even if he wishes to speak a word of truth and to gladden some of his hearers, yet not possessing in himself the word of God in power and reality but only repeating from memory and borrowing words from various parts of the book of Scripture, or what he has heard from spiritual men, and relating and teaching this—see, he seems to gladden others, and others delight in what he tells them but after he has gone through it, each word goes back to the source from which it was taken, and he himself remains once more naked and poor, having no treasure of the Spirit for his own upon which he draws to gladden others, not being himself first gladdened, nor rejoicing in the Spirit.

6. For this reason we should first seek from God with pain of heart and in faith, that He would grant us to find this wealth, the true treasure of Christ in our hearts, in the power and effectual working of the Spirit. In this way, first finding in ourselves the Lord to be our profit and salvation and eternal life, we may then profit others also, according to our strength and opportunity, drawing upon Christ, the treasure within, for all goodness of spiritual words and setting forth mysteries of heaven.

Homily XIX

1. The man who desires to come to the Lord and to be found worthy of eternal life . . . should force himself to every good work and to fulfilling all the commandments of the Lord because of sin that is present with him. For instance, let him force himself to humility of mind in sight of all men and to consider himself less and worse than they, not seeking honor, or praise, or the glory of men from anyone, as it is written in the Gospel (John 12:43), but always having the Lord only before his eyes and His commandments, desiring to please Him only in the meekness of the heart, as the Lord says, "Learn of Me, because I am meek and lowly in heart, and ye shall find rest unto your souls" (Matt. 11:29).

3. In coming to the Lord, a man must force himself to that which is good, even against the inclination of his heart, continually expecting His mercy with undoubting faith, and force himself to love when he has no love; force himself to meekness when he has no meekness; force himself to pity and to have a merciful heart; force himself to be looked down upon, and when he is looked down upon to bear it patiently (to be great-hearted), and when he is made light of or put to shame not to be angry, as it is said, "Beloved, avenge not yourselves" (Rom. 12:19); to force himself to prayer when he has not spiritual prayer; and thus God, beholding him thus striving and compelling himself by force,

in spite of an unwilling heart, gives him the true prayer of the Spirit, gives him true love, meekness, "bowels of mercies" (Col. 3:12), true kindness, and in short, fills him with spiritual fruit.

4. But if a man forces himself only to prayer when he has no prayer, that he may obtain the grace of prayer, but will not force himself to meekness and humility and love and the rest of the Lord's commandments, and takes no pains or trouble or striving to succeed in these; then, to the measure of his purpose and free will, sometimes a grace of prayer is given him, in part, with refreshment and gladness from the Spirit, according to his asking; but in character he is like what he was before. He has no meekness, because he did not seek it with pains, or prepare himself beforehand to become so. He has no humility, because he did not ask for it or force himself to it. He has not love towards all men, because he had no concern or striving about it in his asking for prayer; and in the accomplishment of his work, he has no faith and trust in God, because he knew himself but did not discover that he was without it, or take trouble with pain, seeking from the Lord to obtain firm faith towards Him and a real trust.

6. To all these things must a man force himself, who desires to approve himself to Christ and to please Him in order that the Lord, seeing his earnestness and good will in compelling himself thus to all goodness and simplicity, and kindness and humility of wisdom, and love and prayers, and driving himself to them by force, may give him His whole self—the Lord Himself in truth doing all these things purely in him without labor or forcing, which before he could not do even by force because of sin that was with him; and all the practices of virtue come to him like nature. For from that time onward, the Lord coming and dwelling in him, and he in Him, Himself performs in him His own commandments, without effort, filling him with the fruits of the Spirit. But if a man forces himself only to prayer until he shall receive a gift of it from God, but does not in like manner

force and compel and accustom himself to these other things, he cannot in truth perform them purely and faultlessly.

8. The Spirit Himself bestows these things upon him and teaches him true prayer, true charity, true meekness, to which before he forced himself, and sought for them, and cared for them, and reflected on them, and they were given him; and having thus grown up and been perfected in God, he is permitted to become an heir of the Kingdom, because the humble never falls.

Homily XX

3. If anyone takes a stand on his own righteousness alone, and thinks to redeem himself, he labors in vain and to no purpose. For every self-opinion of one's own righteousness in the last day will be manifested as nothing but filthy rags, as the Prophet Isaiah says: "All our righteousness is as filthy rags" (Is. 64:6).

5. Man is so sore wounded that none can cure him but the Lord only. To Him alone it is possible. He came and "took away the sin of the world" (John 1:29), that is, He dried up the unclean fountain of the thoughts of the soul.

6. Moses came, but he could not bestow a complete cure. Priests, gifts, tithes, sabbaths, new-moons, washings, sacrifices, whole burnt offerings, and every other righteousness, was performed under the law, and the soul could not get cured and cleansed from the unclean issue of bad thoughts. Every righteousness of the soul was unavailing to heal man, until the Savior came, the true Physician, Who cures freely, Who gave Himself a ransom for mankind. He alone accomplished the great, saving deliverance and cure of the soul. He set it free from bondage and brought it out of darkness, glorifying it with His own light. He dried up the fountain of unclean thoughts that was in it. For it is said: "Behold the Lamb of God, that taketh away the sin of the world" (John 1:29).

7. The soul, even though wounded by the wounds of shameful passions, even though blinded by the darkness of sin, yet has the power of will to cry out and call to Jesus, that He might come and work eternal deliverance for the soul.   8. Had not that blind man cried out, had not that sick woman come to the Lord, they would not have found cure; so, unless a man comes to the Lord of his own free will and with whole purpose of heart, and begs Him with un-doubting faith, he will not receive healing. . . . It is because of our unbelief, because of our divided mind, because we do not love Him with all the heart, nor truly believe in Him, that we have not yet found spiritual healing and salvation.

TROPARION TO ST. MACARIUS THE GREAT
Tone 1

A desert-dweller and an angel in the flesh,* and a wonder-worker didst thou reveal thyself, our God-bearing Father Macarius:* by fasting, vigils, and prayer receiving heavenly gifts,* thou healest the infirmities and the souls of those who come with faith to thee.* Glory to Him Who gave thee strength,* glory to Him Who crowned thee,* glory to Him Who works healings to all through thee.

KONTAKION, Tone 4

The Lord placed thee in the house of discipline* as a star enlightening the ends of the earth;* thou didst settle in the desert as in a city,* and receive from God the grace to work miracles.* We venerate thee, Macarius, Father of Fathers.

INDEX

NAMES AND TITLES

SUBJECTS

SCRIPTURE REFERENCES

Drawing of Sts. Barsanuphius and John from the 1892 Russian
edition of *Guidance Toward Spiritual Life*, Moscow.